LITERAT

WILLIAM SHAKESPEARE's

HAMLET

Written by SHAUN McCAF
WITH TONY BUZAN

BARRON'S

Cover photograph © David Cooper—Photostage
Mind Maps: Buzan Centres Ltd.
Illustrations: David Ashby

First edition for the United States and Canada published by
Barron's Educational Series, Inc., 2001.

First published in the United Kingdom by Hodder & Stoughton
Ltd. under the title: *Teach Yourself Literature Guides: Hamlet*

American text edited by Elizabeth Schmid.

All inquiries should be addressed to:
Barron's Educational Series, Inc.
250 Wireless Boulevard
Hauppauge, New York 11788
http://www.barronseduc.com

International Standard Book No. 0-7641-2065-4

Library of Congress Catalog Card No. 2001090180

PRINTED IN THE UNITED STATES OF AMERICA

9 8 7 6 5 4 3 2 1

CONTENTS

How to study   **v**

How to use this guide   **xiii**

Key to icons   **xiv**

Context   **1**
- Sources   1
- What is "revenge tragedy"?   3
- The text   5
- "Back-story"   6

The story of *Hamlet*   **8**

Characterization   **11**

The royal family:
- Hamlet: *I am but mad north-north-west*   11
- Claudius: *smiling, damned villain*   15
- Gertrude: *most seeming-virtuous queen*   17
- The Ghost: *spirit of health or goblin damned*   18

The chief statesman's family:
- Polonius: *a man faithful and honorable*   19
- Laertes: *a very noble youth*   22
- Ophelia: *divided from herself*   23

Others:
- Horatio: *more antique Roman than a Dane*   24
- Rosencrantz and Guildenstern: *those bearers put to sudden death*   25
- Osrick: *a waterfly*   26
- Fortinbras: *I have some rights of memory in this kingdom*   26

Themes   **29**
- Revenge   30
- Words and actions   30

- Madness — 31
- Corruption — 32
- Mortality — 33
- Theater — 33

Language, style, and structure — 36
- Poetry and prose — 36
- Imagery — 38
- Structure — 39

Commentary — 41
- Act 1 — 41
- Act 2 — 50
- Act 3 — 58
- Act 4 — 74
- Act 5 — 82

Critical approaches — 93

Textual analysis — 98

How to get an "A" in English Literature — 102

The exam essay — 103

Model answer and essay plan — 104

Glossary of literary terms — 110

Index — 113

Important Note to Students About Line References

Line references are to The New Folger Library edition of Shakespeare's *Hamlet*. If you have another edition, the line numbers may vary slightly from those provided in this book, although the act and scene numbers should be the same. The line number references from the New Folger edition have been provided to help direct you to specific parts of the play, but often will not be an exact match for line numbers in other editions.

You are now at a very important educational stage of your life, and are probably about to take exams and standardized tests that will have a major impact on your choice of colleges, future career, and goals. This can be an anxious time for many students.

At this crucial stage of your life the one thing you need even more than subject knowledge is the knowledge of *how* to remember, *how* to comprehend, *how* to study, *how* to take notes, and *how* to organize your thoughts. You need to know how to *think*; you need a basic introduction on how to use that super bio-computer inside your head—your brain.

The following pages contain a gold mine of information on how you can achieve success both at school and in your English literature exams, as well as in your professional or college career. These pages will give you skills that will enable you to be successful in *all* your academic pursuits. You will learn:

◆ How to recall more *while* you are learning.
◆ How to recall more *after* you have finished a class or a study period.
◆ How to use special techniques to improve your memory.
◆ How to use a revolutionary note-taking technique called Mind Maps that will double your memory and help you to write essays and answer exam questions.
◆ How to prepare for tests and exams.

How to understand, improve, and master your memory of English Literature

Your memory really is like a muscle. Don't exercise it and it will grow weaker; *do* exercise it properly and it will grow incredibly more powerful. There are really only four main things you need to understand about your memory in order to increase its power dramatically:

Recall during learning
– THE NEED FOR BREAKS!

When you are studying, your memory can concentrate, understand, and recall well for between 20 and 45 minutes at a time. Then it *needs* a  break. If you continue for longer than this without one, your memory starts to break down. If you study for hours nonstop, you will remember only a fraction of what you have been trying to learn, and you will have wasted valuable review time.

So, ideally, *study for less than an hour*, then take a five- to ten-minute break. During this break listen to music, go for a walk, do some exercise, or just daydream. (Daydreaming is a necessary brain-power booster—geniuses do it regularly.) During the break your brain will be sorting out what it has been learning and you will go back to your books with the new information safely stored and organized in your memory. We recommend breaks at regular intervals as you work through this book. Make sure you take them!

Recall after learning
– THE WAVES OF YOUR MEMORY

What do you think begins to happen to your memory right *after* you have finished learning something? Does it immediately start forgetting? No! Surprisingly, your brain actually *increases* its power and continues remembering. For a short time after your study session, your brain integrates the information, making a more complete picture of everything it has just learned. Only then does the rapid decline in memory begin, as much as 80 percent of what you have learned can be forgotten in a day.

However, if you catch the top of the wave of your memory, and briefly review what you have been studying at the correct time, the memory is imprinted far more strongly, and stays at the crest of the wave for a much longer time. To maximize your brain's power to remember, take a few minutes at the end of a day and use a Mind Map to review what you have learned. Then review it at the end of a week, again at the end of a month, and finally a week before your test or exam. That way you'll ride your memory wave all the way to your exam, success, and beyond!

The memory principle of association

The muscle of your memory becomes stronger when it can **associate**—when it can link things together.

Think about your best friend, and all the things your mind *automatically* links with that person. Think about your favorite hobby, and all the associations your mind has when you think about (remember!) that hobby.

When you are studying, use this memory principle to make associations between the elements in your subjects, and thus to improve both your memory and your chances of success.

The memory principle of imagination

The muscle of your memory will improve significantly if you can produce big images in your mind. Rather than just memorizing the name of a character, imagine that character of the novel or play as if you were a video producer filming that person's life. The same goes for images in poetry.

In *all* your subjects use the **imagination** memory principle.

Throughout this book you will find special association and imagination techniques (called mnemonics after the Greek goddess Mnemosyne) that will make it much easier for you to remember the topic being discussed. Look for them!

Your new success formula: Mind Maps®

You have noticed that when people go on vacations, or travel, they take maps. Why? To give them a general picture of where they are going, to help them locate places of special interest and importance, to help them find things more easily, and to help them remember distances and locations, etc.

It is exactly the same with your mind and with study. If you have a "map of the territory" of what you have to learn, then everything is easier. In learning and study, the Mind Map is that special tool.

As well as helping you with all areas of study, the Mind Map actually *mirrors the way your brain works.* Your Mind Maps can be used for taking notes from your books, for taking notes in class, for preparing your homework, for presenting your homework, for reviewing your tests, for checking your and your friends' knowledge in any subject, and for *helping you understand anything you learn.* Mind Maps are especially useful in English literature, as they allow you to map out the whole territory of a novel, play or poem, giving you an "at-a-glance" snapshot of all the key information you need to know.

The Mind Maps throughout this book use **imagination** and **association**. As such, they automatically strengthen your memory muscle every time you use them. You will find Mind Maps in this book that summarize the most important points about the characters and plot sequences in *Hamlet*. Study these Mind Maps, add some color, personalize them, and then try drawing your own Mind Maps—you will remember them far better! Put them on your walls and in your files for a quick-and-easy review. Mind Maps are fast, efficient, effective, and, importantly, *fun* to do!

HOW TO DRAW A MIND MAP

1 Start in the middle of the page with the page turned sideways. This gives your brain more radiant freedom for its thoughts.

2 Always start by drawing a picture or symbol of the book or its title. Why? Because *a picture is worth a thousand words to your brain.* Try to use at least three colors, as color helps your memory even more.

3 Let your thoughts flow, and write or draw your ideas on colored branching lines connected to your central image. The key symbols and words are the headings for your topic. The Mind Map at the top of the next page shows you how to start.

4 Next, add facts and ideas by drawing more, smaller, branches on to the appropriate main branches, just like a tree.

5 Always print your word clearly on its line. Use only one word per line.

6 To link ideas and thoughts on different branches, use arrows, colors, underlining, and boxes.

HOW TO READ A MIND MAP

1 Begin in the center, the focus of your novel, play, or poem.

2 The words/images attached to the center are like chapter headings; read them next.

3 Always read out from the center, in every direction (even on the left-hand side, where you will read from right to left, instead of the usual left to right).

USING MIND MAPS

Mind Maps are a versatile tool—use them for taking notes in class or from books, for solving problems, for brainstorming with friends, and for reviewing for exams—their uses are infinite! You will find them invaluable for planning essays for coursework and exams. Number your main branches in the order in which you want to use them and off you go—the main headings for your essay are done and all your ideas are logically organized!

HOW TO MAKE STUDY EASY FOR YOUR BRAIN

When you are going somewhere, is it easier to know beforehand where you are going, or not? Obviously it is easier if you *do* know. It is the same for your brain and a book. When you get a new book, there are seven things you can do to help your brain get to "know the territory" faster:

1 Scan through the whole book in less than 20 minutes, as you would if you were in a store deciding whether or not to buy it. This gives your brain *control.*

2 Think about what you already know about the subject. You'll often find out it's a lot more than you thought. A good way of doing this is to do a quick Mind Map on *everything you know* after you have skimmed through the book.

3 Ask who, what, why, where, when, and how questions about what is in the book. Questions help your brain "fish" the knowledge out.

4 Ask your friends what they know about the subject. This helps them review the knowledge in their own brains, and helps your brain get new knowledge about what you are studying.

5 Quickly read through the book again, this time looking for any diagrams, pictures, and illustrations, and also at the beginnings and ends of chapters. Most information is contained in the beginnings and ends.

6 If you come across any difficult parts in your book, mark them and *move on.* Your brain *will* be able to solve the problems when you come back to them a little later. Much like saving the difficult parts of a jigsaw puzzle for later. When you have finished the book, quickly review it one more time and then discuss it with friends. This will lodge it permanently in your memory.

7 Create a Mind Map as you study the book. This helps your brain to organize and hold (remember!) information as you study.

Preparing for tests and exams

◆ To avoid **exam panic** study hard at the beginning of your course, not the end. It takes the same amount of time, so you may as well use it where it is best placed!

◆ Use Mind Maps throughout your course, and build a Master Mind Map for each subject—a giant Mind Map that summarizes everything you know about the subject.

◆ Use memory techniques such as mnemonics (verses or systems for remembering things like dates and events or lists).

◆ Get together with one or two friends to study, compare Mind Maps, and discuss topics.

AND FINALLY...

◆ *Have fun while you learn*—studies show that those people who enjoy what they are doing understand and remember it more, and generally do better.

◆ *Use your teachers* as resource centers. Ask them for help with specific topics and with more general advice on how you can improve your all-around performance.

◆ *Personalize your* **Literature Made Easy** *book* by underlining and highlighting, by adding notes and pictures. Allow your brain to have a conversation with it!

Your amazing brain and its amazing cells

Your brain is like a super, *super, SUPER* computer. The world's best computers have only a few thousand or hundred thousand computer chips. Your brain has "computer chips" too, and they are called brain cells. Unlike the computer, you do not have only a few thousand computer chips—the number of brain cells in your head is a *million MILLION*!! This means you are a genius just waiting to discover yourself! All you have to do is learn how to get those brain cells working together, and you'll not only become a better student, you'll have more free time to pursue your other fun activities.

The more you understand your amazing brain the more it will repay and amaze you! I wish you and your brain every success.

(Tony Buzan)

HOW TO USE THIS GUIDE

This guide assumes that you have already read *Hamlet,*
although you could read Context and The story of *Hamlet* first.
It is best to use the guide alongside the play. You could read
the Characterization and Themes sections without referring to
it, but you will get more out of these if you do.

The sections

The Commentary section can be used in a number of ways.
One way is to read a scene of the play, and then read the
relevant commentary. Continue until you come to a test
section, test yourself—then take a break! Alternatively, read the
Commentary for a scene, then read that scene in the play, then
go back to the Commentary. See what works best for you.

Critical approaches sums up the main critical views and
interpretations of the play. Your own response is important, but
be aware of these approaches too.

How to get an "A" in English Literature gives valuable advice
on what to look for in a novel or play, and what skills you
need to develop in order to achieve your personal best.

The exam essay is a useful "night before" reminder of how to
tackle exam questions, though it will help you more if you
also look at it much earlier in the year. Model answer gives an
example of an A-grade essay and the Mind Map and plan used
to write it.

The questions

Whenever you come across a question in the guide with a
star ✪ in front of it, think about it for a moment. You could
make a Mini Mind Map or a few notes to focus your mind.
There is not usually a "right" answer to these: it is important
for you to develop your own opinions if you want to get an
"A." The Test sections are designed to take you about 15–20
minutes each—which will be time well spent. Take a short
break after each one.

KEY TO ICONS

Whenever a **theme**—an idea explored by the author—is dealt with in the guide, an appropriate icon is used. This means you can find where a theme is mentioned by flicking through the book. *Hamlet* is a play with several key themes, of which revenge is the most important. The plot is driven by Hamlet's desire for revenge upon Claudius, and all other themes are secondary to this. It is Shakespeare's genius in dealing with "big" themes in his plots that make his plays timeless.

Six themes in all are identified by icons in the Characterization and Commentary sections. These icons will help you get an understanding of the play. The themes are explained in depth in the Themes section.

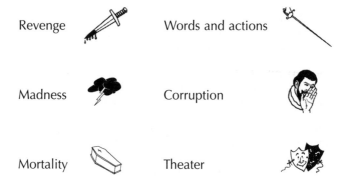

Revenge   Words and actions

Madness   Corruption

Mortality   Theater

LANGUAGE, STYLE, AND STRUCTURE

This icon is used in the Commentary wherever there is a special focus on the author's choice of words and imagery.

Sources

Most of Shakespeare's plays were based on existing sources, on stories that had already been written down, and sometimes made into plays. But Shakespeare's genius turned these basic stories into something new and far greater. Compared to his plays, Shakespeare's sources are the bare bones of plots.

At the end of the twelfth century a Danish chronicler, Saxo Grammaticus, wrote his Latin text *Historiae Danicae*, a collection of his country's "histories" and legends. These stories were already ancient when he wrote them down, 300 years before Shakespeare began work on *Hamlet*.

The most famous story in Saxo's collection is of Amleth, son of Horwendil. Horwendil ruled Jutland (in Denmark) jointly with his brother Feng (or Fengo). Feng murders his brother, takes control of the kingdom, and marries Horwendil's widow Gerutha. The young Amleth fears that Feng might try to make a clean sweep and murder him too, so he pretends to be mad and thereby harmless. The ploy works. Amleth is allowed to grow up unmolested. But gradually Feng begins to suspect that Amleth is acting. He tries to lure Amleth into confessing his secret to a beautiful girl. Then a friend of Feng's spies on Amleth when he is in private conversation with Gerutha. Amleth kills him, dismembers the body, and hides it.

Now desperate, Feng sends Amleth to England guarded by two servants bearing Amleth's death warrant. Amleth gets hold of their warrant while they are asleep and changes the name from his to those of the two servants. He marries the King of England's daughter and later returns to Jutland. He has previously told Gerutha to hold a service of remembrance for him twelve months after he left Jutland. He arrives back in the middle of this service and kills Feng.

❂ How do the characters in the legend of Amleth match those in *Hamlet*? (You could make a list.)

Although key elements of Shakespeare's play are missing from this bare plot (there is no ghost as the murder is enacted in

Saxo's story), the main theme of revenge and several key steps in Amleth's/Hamlet's journey to achieving it are in Saxo's tale. But two things are vastly different in Shakespeare's work: the character of Hamlet is phenomenally sophisticated and complex, and the world of Elsinore is not the crude society of Dark Ages Denmark but a court that Elizabethans would recognize as almost part of their own world.

There is also, amazingly perhaps when you consider the eight deaths in *Hamlet,* more straightforward violence in Saxo's tale. The beautiful girl is brutally treated by Amleth. On his return to Jutland, Amleth burns down the hall with all the drunken courtiers inside before going off to murder Feng! Saxo's story was locked into a dark and primitive world far removed from Shakespeare's Renaissance London. Nonetheless, writers saw something universal and exciting in the basic plot of the Amleth story.

Shakespeare may never have read Saxo, but he could have had access to a more readily available version of the tale, in the popular *Histoires Tragiques* series written by the Frenchman Belleforest and published between 1559 and 1582. In his fifth collection, published in 1570, approximately thirty years before the first performance of *Hamlet,* Belleforest tells a more sophisticated version of the Amleth story. Things move closer to Shakespeare's plot in that the girl sent to discover Amleth's secret is his childhood sweetheart, like Ophelia. But Belleforest still has a hero who is a simple revenger, not the enormously complex intellectual figure that Shakespeare creates in his character of Hamlet.

The third key source for Shakespeare's greatest drama is another Elizabethan play—but it has been lost! Scholars have long speculated over the author and content of what has become known as the *Ur-Hamlet* ("Ur" means earliest). What is certain (from comments and records of people who went to see it) is that it was being performed in the 1590s and that it added a ghost to the Amleth plot. The author of the lost *Ur-Hamlet* was probably Thomas Kyd, a playwright who produced a great revenge tragedy, *The Spanish Tragedy,* in 1587. Kyd was writing at the time the *Ur-Hamlet* appeared and he had the interest and skill to produce a revenge tragedy based on the Amleth story. In the first, "bad," edition of Shakespeare's plays (see The text, p. 5) a version of *Hamlet* is printed that seems to have sections drawn in from another work, probably the mysterious *Ur-Hamlet*.

The bare bones of the story of *Hamlet* had been in existence for hundreds of years. There was an active tradition of revenge plays in Elizabethan theater, but *Hamlet* is much greater than any other play of the revenge genre.

What is "revenge tragedy"?

Revenge tragedies were a type of play that flourished on the Elizabethan and Jacobean stage. Their plots usually shared a number of common elements:

- a hero who learns of an act that requires vengeance from the ghost or spirit of a murdered family member;
- scenes of feigned (or genuine) madness;
- a play within a play;
- a graveyard scene;
- plenty of physical violence and death!

Hamlet clearly has all these key ingredients.

Most importantly the hero is caught in a web that means he condemns himself when he (revengers were exclusively male!) finally carries out the revenge, so he too is damned and killed. Many revenge tragedies were pretty straightforward popular entertainments stringing together these basic ingredients, but Shakespeare took these elements and wrote something that far exceeded the scope of any other play of the revenge tragedy genre (or "tragedy of the blood" as it was also known). Shakespeare had already written three plays that feature revenge as the main or at least crucial element of their plots before *Hamlet*: *Titus Andronicus, Romeo and Juliet* and *Julius Caesar*. Probably only Thomas Kyd's *The Spanish Tragedy* and Christopher Marlowe's *The Jew of Malta* come anywhere near *Hamlet* in terms of skillful writing and depth of characterization.

REVENGE TRAGEDY INGREDIENTS

- GHOST OF A MURDERED FAMILY MEMBER
- SCENES OF MADNESS
- A PLAY WITHIN A PLAY
- A GRAVEYARD SCENE
- PHYSICAL VIOLENCE AND DEATH

The text

There was a first printed version of *Hamlet* in 1603, which scholars now refer to as the "bad" quarto. (*Quarto* refers to the page size, basically small and square.) It is bad because, compared to later versions of the play, it seems to be full of errors and omissions. It was an unauthorized printing of the play. The printer did not have access to Shakespeare's original papers. It is thought that it was dictated from memory by an actor who probably played Marcellus, because this minor part is very faithfully reproduced. But other characters are not well remembered and often just the sense of what a scene or speech is about is conveyed with a few key lines recalled. All the events in the plot are included, but it seems the person dictating the play made up his own run-of-the-mill verse to fill gaps in his memory. This first quarto has about 2,200 lines, whereas in the second, or "good," quarto, the play runs to over 3,800 lines.

This second quarto appeared in 1604–1605 and contains the longest version of *Hamlet.* The printer claimed it was a *true and perfect copy*, suggesting he had worked from Shakespeare's original papers. But it is badly printed, with many errors: Shakespeare's handwriting is hard to read!

In 1623, after Shakespeare's death, the first folio of plays appeared. (*Folio* again refers to page size, tall and narrow.) The version of *Hamlet* it contains is slightly shorter than the good quarto, but with many obvious errors and inconsistencies cleared up. It has better stage directions, suggesting that this version represents the best account we have of how the play was performed in Shakespeare's time.

Remember that *Hamlet* was written to be performed. Lines would have been cut in rehearsals to make the production work, to suit actor's styles, etc. If you see a production of *Hamlet* today you will almost certainly find that the director has made cuts. It is the longest Shakespeare play, and an uncut version—running to over three hours in length—can be a test of stamina!

Check which version of the play you are studying. The references throughout this guide refer to The New Folger Library Shakespeare edition (1992).

"Back-story"

Many plots require explanation of events that are imagined to have occurred before the play, novel, or film actually begins. In drama, back-story is often necessary because the space available to tell a story is limited to what an audience can watch in an evening. In the case of *Hamlet* it was hard enough to get such a long play squeezed into the daylight hours available in an afternoon at an Elizabethan theater.

There are many ways in which a writer can work relevant back-story into the plot. In *Hamlet*, Shakespeare has to get in some important information about Old Hamlet, the king who is now a ghost. He does this with just a few clues, which you should pick up in order to understand the situation at court and for Hamlet personally at the start of the play. These are found in Act 1, scenes 1 and 2.

What has happened before the play begins? Hamlet has been away at the university in Wittenburg. Claudius's court appears to be a politically smooth and civilized operation. Voltemand and Cornelius are sent to negotiate with Norway like modern ambassadors. But Old Hamlet engaged in physical combat with Old Fortinbras of Norway. Horatio describes (Act 1, scene 1, lines 73–74) the old king and how he *in an angry parle/ Smote the sleded poleaxe on the ice.* Contrast this dark, heroic image with the fact that in court they now exercise by dueling with light rapiers. The ghost underlines this change when he appears in full battle armor: *He wore his beaver up* (Act 1, scene 2, line 245)—a beaver being the hinged faceguard on a battle helmet. Claudius dismisses swordsmanship as a pastime *Of the unworthiest siege...A very riband in the cap of youth* (Act 4, scene 7, lines 86–88).

The differences hinted at between the way Old Hamlet ruled and the current state of affairs suggest a shift from an old, dark but possibly heroic and chivalrous world, to a more modern, sophisticated but scheming and dishonest one. If Claudius has achieved this we might commend him, but with only a few months having elapsed between the old king's death and the start of the play, it is probably more a case of the world changing, becoming less wild, less governed by feats of individual valor and violence. But Claudius does represent a new way of operating: Old Hamlet with his physical force and battle armor was the last of a dying world.

Hamlet's hatred of Claudius and the court at Elsinore may be colored by his regretting the passing of this old order in which his father was a hero. Hamlet admits to being *no Hercules*, but he is none the less a good swordsman and readily takes on Laertes (albeit in a supposedly sporting bout with blunted swords). Otherwise he displays none of the physical skills needed in that old world his father ruled: he is too intellectual and reflective. It is important to be aware that this dark shadow of a bygone world hangs over the play and over Hamlet in the form of his father's ghost. When Hamlet says of his father, *I shall not look upon his like again* (Act 1, scene 2, line 196), he is choosing his words carefully.

There are several problems with the back-story to the play. What is the history of the relationship (if any) between Ophelia and Hamlet? How long has she known him? Since childhood presumably, as her father has been part of the court for years. So when did Hamlet start making overtures to her? If he has been away in Wittenburg, then probably only during the few weeks he has been back following his father's death. These unclear small points confuse the scenes between Hamlet and Ophelia. And why has Hamlet not naturally inherited the kingdom from his father? Why has it passed to an uncle?

THE STORY OF *HAMLET*

Warlike Old Hamlet, King of Denmark, has died. His Ghost has been seen on the battlements of the castle at Elsinore. Claudius, the dead king's brother, has inherited the throne and married Gertrude, his widow. Claudius appears to preside happily and skillfully over a united court. Only Prince Hamlet seems unhappy, still mourning the father he idolized.

Hamlet is present at the Ghost's second appearance. It tells Hamlet that it is his father's spirit and that he was murdered by Claudius. Hamlet must revenge the murder by killing Claudius. Meanwhile Ophelia, daughter of the court's chief counselor Polonius, is told to break off any romantic relationship she may have with Hamlet. Her brother Laertes leaves for Paris.

Act 2 takes place some weeks after these events. Hamlet's behavior suggests he has gone mad, though he has hinted privately that this may be a ruse. Claudius has sent for Hamlet's college friends, Rosencrantz and Guildenstern, to get them to find out what is wrong. Polonius tells the king and queen that Hamlet's madness is caused by unfulfilled love for Ophelia. They plan to set up an "accidental" meeting between Hamlet and Ophelia, on which the king and Polonius will eavesdrop.

Rosencrantz and Guildenstern confess to Hamlet that they were sent for. The Players arrive, much to Hamlet's delight. He calls for the First Player to give a speech. The actor moves himself to tears. This prompts Hamlet's soliloquy in which he curses himself for having less passion for revenge than the actor expresses for fictional characters. With the Players he hatches a plot for them to perform a play that contains a murder very much like the one Claudius committed. His reaction will test the truth of what the Ghost has told Hamlet.

The famous *To be or not to be* soliloquy precedes Hamlet's meeting with Ophelia. Hamlet realizes she is colluding in the eavesdropping and flies into a "mad" rage against her and the weakness of her sex. The king decides to pack Hamlet off to England.

In the evening of the same day the "play within a play" is performed before the court. Hamlet displays a mad enthusiasm for the performance, acting as commentator on events. At the depiction of the murder, Claudius storms out. Alone with Horatio, Hamlet decides that Claudius is guilty of murder. The queen calls Hamlet to visit her in her chamber. On the way he comes across the king praying. Hamlet does not hear him confess to the murder, nor to the tortures of guilt he suffers. Hamlet does not kill him although it is a perfect opportunity. The king is praying, and he may escape hell if he dies now.

Polonius has hidden himself in the queen's room to overhear her meeting with Hamlet. Frightened by Hamlet's aggression she calls out. Polonius also cries out and Hamlet stabs him through a curtain, thinking it is the king. Hamlet forces the queen to confront her wrongs in marrying her first husband's brother. When Hamlet again becomes angry the Ghost appears to caution him. But the queen cannot see the Ghost and she thinks Hamlet is mad. Hamlet leaves, taking Polonius's body, which he hides in the castle.

Rosencrantz and Guildenstern chase Hamlet and bring him to the king. He is despatched to England immediately, with them as guards. They are carrying his death warrant. On the way he encounters Fortinbras's army marching to fight a pointless battle with the Poles.

Ophelia wanders through the court. She has been driven mad by the death of her father. Laertes returns, furiously seeking revenge. Claudius convinces him that Hamlet is to blame. Ophelia makes a second appearance and Laertes is driven into a frenzy of revenge again. Claudius and Laertes begin to form an alliance against Hamlet.

Horatio receives a letter from Hamlet explaining that he has escaped and is back in Denmark. Claudius and Laertes plot Hamlet's death in a rigged fencing match, with one sharpened and poisoned sword and a poisoned drink. Gertrude brings news that Ophelia has drowned.

The final Act begins with a comic exchange between Hamlet and a gravedigger who is preparing a grave. Hamlet meditates on mortality over the skull of Yorick, a court jester whom he knew in his boyhood. Ophelia's funeral arrives. Hamlet and

Horatio hide. Laertes's exaggerated grief so infuriates Hamlet that he bursts out and challenges Laertes. They fight over Ophelia's grave.

Back in the castle Hamlet tells Horatio how he returned and that he altered the death warrant. Rosencrantz and Guildenstern are now the victims. Osrick arrives and invites Hamlet to take part in the "sporting" fencing match against Laertes. Hamlet senses something is wrong but accepts. He appears resigned to whatever fate has in store, even death.

The climax of the play is the fencing match before the king and queen. In the heat of the bout swords are swapped and both Hamlet and Laertes are wounded and poisoned. Gertrude drinks the poisoned drink. Laertes tells Hamlet all this carnage is Claudius's doing. Hamlet finally gains revenge by killing Claudius. Hamlet dies in Horatio's arms. Fortinbras arrives and assumes the throne of Denmark.

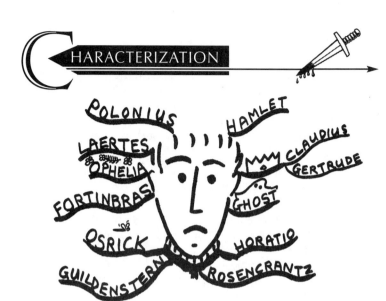

CHARACTERIZATION

The Mini Mind Map above summarizes the main characters in *Hamlet*. When you have read this section, look at the full Mind Map on p. 28, then make a copy of the Mini Mind Map and try to add to it from memory.

> **Hamlet:** *I am but mad north-north-west*

Hamlet is so much about the nature of its main character that it is impossible to discuss the drama without describing in great detail the character of the Prince of Denmark. The Commentary section of this guide helps you think about the motivations, emotions and predispositions of Hamlet throughout the play. Read the Commentary carefully to build up your idea of how Hamlet's character can be determined by what he says and does. There has been so much critical analysis of him that there are alternative theories for almost everything he does (and doesn't!) do. Often, the Commentary offers you alternative interpretations of his words and actions, leaving you to make up your own mind about Hamlet's character.

This section offers you more general ideas to consider about Hamlet's character. They are not a character description: they are based on questions that critics have asked about Shakespeare's most famous character.

HAMLET'S RESUMÉ

A class of fifteen students may well have fifteen different impressions of Hamlet's character. You can hold any opinion you want on the true nature of Hamlet, so long as you can provide quotes from the text to support your case. But there are some undisputed facts about him, upon which you can develop your ideas about the more ambiguous elements of his personality:

- He is intellectual, well educated, and able to think and express complex thoughts.
- He is a knowledgeable supporter of theater.
- He is liked by the common people and able to discourse with them easily and on almost equal terms.
- But he can "pull rank" as a prince when it suits him.
- He can be ruthless.
- His studies at the university have not stopped him from practicing his swordsmanship.
- He was well liked by other students.

✪ Find a piece of evidence from the play to support each of these facts about Hamlet. (His ruthlessness, for example, is demonstrated by his rewriting the warrant that consigns Rosencrantz and Guildenstern to their deaths.)

HAMLET'S HESITATION

The most frequently asked question about Hamlet is "Why does he take so long to kill Claudius?" Critics have suggested various theories for his hesitation. One view sees Hamlet as a romantic figure, a naturally pure and honest soul who lacks the simple violent drive of a hero. Even a quick reading of the play shows this idea to be pretty wide of the mark, but it does contain some truth. Compared to the bloodthirsty revengers of simpler revenge tragedies, Hamlet does have a more analytical, perhaps more gentle, approach to life.

Another school of thought explains Hamlet's hesitations and self-doubts in terms of his unnaturally affectionate relationship with his mother. If Hamlet is himself aware of the excessive degree of love he shows his mother, then he could doubt the motives he may have to act against her husband. He may recognize in himself a dangerous tendency to view Claudius not only as his father's murderer but as a successful rival for his mother's affections. It is not helpful to explain

Hamlet's behavior purely in terms of an Oedipus complex, but it is interesting to look at his actions in this light.

MADNESS OR MELANCHOLY?

Hamlet assumes madness as a device to pursue his revenge, but is he ever actually mad? Even at the point where real madness seems most likely, in the "closet" scene (Act 3, scene 4), his actions are still directed towards his sworn purpose. He kills Polonius thinking him to be Claudius. He offers his mother (Oedipus complex notwithstanding) advice which he genuinely believes to have value and through which he can explain his opinion of her and of Claudius.

✪ Hamlet's madness could all be feigned. Look through the play carefully and see what he might hope to achieve by each display of *wild and whirling words*. Polonius, Ophelia, and Claudius are the chief recipients of his displays of insanity: what end is he trying to achieve when he encounters each of these characters?

But if Hamlet does actually lose his sanity, where does this happen and for how long? Is his miraculous transformation in Act 5 a sudden return to sanity from genuine madness? Think about what effect on the drama real madness would have. Would it diminish the power and resonance of Hamlet's words and actions?

Hamlet undoubtedly is afflicted with the lesser mental condition of melancholy. He tells us right at the start of the play (in his soliloquy in Act 1, scene 2) that he is in such a low state that he would consider killing himself had not God *fixed/ His canon 'gainst self-slaughter* (lines 135–136). Has this deep depression been caused purely by the death of his father and the rapid remarriage of his mother? Was he a happy, carefree student before these events? Although we might believe that it is recent events in Elsinore that have driven him into melancholy, it is worth noting how often in his soliloquies his gloom encompasses the whole world and everything in it.

HONOR

Hamlet idolizes the memory of his father. Nobility and kingly honor are key elements of this picture of perfection. But does Hamlet possess honor? Does he think it honorable to kill to revenge his father, as the Ghost demands? This is a simple eye-for-an-eye view of honor, and Hamlet appears too much of an analytical intellectual to accept such a primitive code. Yet his hesitations cause him terrible anguish, and one of the elements of his torment is a feeling that he is not doing what is expected of him.

Hamlet does many things that could easily be seen as dishonorable. He treats Ophelia badly; he callously—and carelessly—murders Polonius; he sends Rosencrantz and Guildenstern to their deaths by a trick; and he fights with Laertes at Ophelia's funeral. But it is hard not to finish reading or seeing the play without thinking that in some vital way Hamlet is the most honorable person in the drama. In Act 5 he appears genuinely regretful that he is cast in the role of a revenger. His somewhat strange apology to Laertes does appear heartfelt, if badly timed. His friendship with Horatio seems honest and binding. And above all these practical things there is a sense that Hamlet did the best in a situation where the treachery and violence were not of his making. His hesitation shows that he has, if not honor, a sense of moral responsibility. He is careful to weigh all alternatives to ensure that he acts justly.

WOMEN AND PURITY

Hamlet recalls his father's marriage to Gertrude as an example of wedded bliss; though his perceptions seem a little too intimate for comfort. He dwells reverently (demonstrating Oedipal tendencies no doubt) on the joy of their marriage. Female purity and honor are core ingredients in this picture of married bliss. Hamlet appears to look for these qualities in all women. Ophelia is castigated because he feels she lacks them.

✪ Shakespeare lays great significance on the word fair to describe women (see p. 61). Find places where Hamlet uses this word to describe women.

Hamlet's "mad" attack on Ophelia in Act 3, scene 1, is a rant against female depravity and wantonness. Given that he knows Ophelia is a willing collaborator in the deception of this overheard conversation, Hamlet is likely to feel anger toward her. She is a girl to whom he is supposed to have been attracted. But the form this anger takes, dwelling on female weakness and lust, reveals a dark frustration in Hamlet's whole view of women.

However, Hamlet's attitude to women is not as easily summarized as this scene suggests, for in his dalliance with Ophelia before the "play within a play" it is he who is bawdy and sexually suggestive. This could be dismissed as more feigned madness, or it could reveal a passionate but warped sexuality underlying the cool and intellectual Hamlet of the soliloquies.

Claudius: *smiling, damned villain*

Claudius is the only other character in the play to have anything like Hamlet's complexity and depth of character. Unlike the glowering villains of other revenge tragedies, Claudius is a fully rounded human being. The core of his character is a flaw in his personality and the conflict this creates within him. The flaw is that he murdered his brother. The conflict is that he does not want to give up the rewards the murder has brought him.

As with Hamlet, the Commentary section of this guide will help you explore Claudius's character as it is revealed by his role in the drama. These notes are more general points to consider when trying to develop your own picture of Claudius.

Why did he kill his brother? Is it that he simply wanted the crown and Gertrude was just a welcome bonus? Had he always hated his brother? In the Middle Ages the succession of an eldest son to his father's throne was not automatic. There were various systems for electing a new king upon the death of the old. Perhaps Claudius felt that he should have been king instead of his brother all along. Or maybe he murdered because he loved Gertrude and wanted her husband out of the way.

Is Claudius a good king? Is he a well-liked king? The answer to the first question seems to be yes. He runs his court smoothly and efficiently (see Act 1, scene 2). He appears to have moved it on light years from the Dark Ages of his brother's reign, which we glimpse in Horatio's brief memory of old Hamlet with a battleaxe out on the ice parleying with the enemy. ("Parleying" implies a battle just fought or imminent.) Claudius, by contrast, sends an envoy to his potential enemies. No one at court speaks ill of him.

But is Claudius a popular king? When Laertes returns from Paris the *rabble* flock to him as a challenger to the throne.

Laertes has spent considerable time in France, so it seems they are seizing on a fairly remote figure to be their champion. And Claudius claims that he dared not act against Hamlet after Polonius's murder because the Prince is so loved by the *general gender* that they would take his side against the king's. Is it the case that the people of Denmark would prefer anyone to Claudius as their monarch?

Hamlet of course hates Claudius, for what he has done as much as for who he is. Hamlet describes him in a whole range of unfavorable terms and images throughout the play. ✪ What examples can you find of Hamlet expressing his hatred of Claudius through images of decay?

It is not until we hear Claudius's prayer in Act 3, scene 3, that we see the human side of the king, painfully revealed in his self-loathing and suffering. This crucial scene develops many aspects of Claudius's character. We hear from his own lips that he murdered his brother. We see the suffering human behind the veneer of efficient kingship. We cannot help but feel some sympathy for the man, at the very moment when he confesses his crime. Although he never mentions his feelings toward Gertrude he seems ready to suffer the tortures of guilt that hanging on to all he gained from the murder will only increase. Those gains include Gertrude.

Claudius makes a clear journey through the drama of the play. He is increasingly forced to recognize the destructive guilt he will suffer because of the murder he committed. He is pushed to desperate measures partly by Hamlet's poorly focused "campaign" of revenge, partly by his own corrosive guilt. His relationship with Gertrude is a simple barometer of the change in him. Their relationship is never directly spoken of either by them or by anyone else except Hamlet, who naturally despises it. But for most of the play they seem loving and unified. Most productions direct Gertrude to be joyously happy, entering the court smiling and clinging on to the king's arm. Some portray them as downright frisky lovers! But by the end of the play Claudius has been driven by guilt and his own evil machinations to the point where he watches Gertrude drink poison and does not lift a finger to help her. He has reached the bottom of the depths of despair. If he dashes the cup from her lip he reveals his guilt; if he doesn't she will die and he will lose her anyway. But like a cornered animal he will cling to his cover even though he is doomed.

❂ Whose deaths would you say Claudius is primarily responsible for? Make a brief note explaining the king's guilt or implication in the deaths of each of your chosen victims.

Gertrude: *most seeming-virtuous queen*

Most critics would say that, like her second husband, Gertrude is a character whose actions are driven by the pressure of living with guilt. Despite the happiness she displays in the first stages of the drama, she secretly knows her marriage to Claudius is wrong. Elizabethans would have considered it incestuous. The point at which her guilt springs into view, and the line upon which this interpretation of Gertrude is based, comes in the pivotal closet scene, Act 3, scene 4. In words reminiscent of the murderous Lady Macbeth, who sees imaginary indelible blood spots on her hands, Gertrude replies to Hamlet's assault on the propriety of her marriage:

Thou turnest mine eyes into my very soul,
And there I see such black and grained spots
As will not leave their tinct. (lines 100–102)

After this confession we must assume that any support Gertrude shows for Claudius is merely her maintaining appearances to deceive a murderer. We are convinced that, until Hamlet tells her, she has no idea that Claudius murdered her first husband. We assume that after the closet scene she sees Hamlet as not mad but acting. But for what purpose? He doesn't tell her he plans to murder her new husband. Nonetheless, her realizing that her son is not actually mad would in part explain her support of him in the fencing match.

But another interpretation is that Gertrude never wavers in her love and support of Claudius. She supports Hamlet in the match because he is her son. Her affection toward her new husband in the first two and a half Acts seems genuine. Apart from her "confession" quoted above, everything she says in the closet scene could be interpreted as the words of a woman dealing with a crazed homicidal son lecturing her on her sex life. You could argue that the *black and grained spots* appear because Hamlet convinces her only that the manner of her relationship with her husband, not the husband himself, is wrong. He has just finished telling her she's basically too old to be acting like a whore, and this might stain the self-image of a queen whose private life is under constant scrutiny by the court!

Does Hamlet convince his mother that he is sane, that her husband is a murderer and that her marriage is an appalling and unnatural travesty? You will have to make your own mind up. Act 3, scene 4, is the place to look for clues.

The issue is made more difficult by a line of critical thought that defines Gertrude as a woman whose whole character is entirely based on maintaining appearances. She operates as smoothly in the court as Claudius, although she has little to do except support him. As the deaths begin and the court's surface calm shatters, she gives way to stronger, more genuine emotions, primarily sadness. She laments the death of Ophelia and regrets that Hamlet never married her.

If Gertrude is a mistress of concealment then it would explain why she is never given a soliloquy to express her true thoughts and feelings. She is cloaked in an air of mystery. Did she know of the murder? Did she want her first husband dead? She might even have helped dispatch him. That could account for those *black and grained spots.* Gertrude keeps her own counsel, at least until the deaths of Polonius and Ophelia. She may well be only a *most seeming-virtuous queen.*

The Ghost: *spirit of health or goblin damned*

The Ghost is not a character in any true sense, but he is crucial to the drama of the play. His mixed messages to Hamlet from beyond the grave raise the plot from that of a simple revenge tragedy to a complex psychological drama. Typically, a revenge tragedy ghost just points an accusing finger and demands revenge. The Ghost in *Hamlet* gives a far more complex and ambiguous series of messages. Hamlet's responses to these drive the whole of the subsequent revenge drama.

Study the conversation between Hamlet and the Ghost in Act 1, scene 5. The Ghost claims it does not want pity, then it spends lines 14–29 describing the awful sufferings it endures. The Ghost demands Hamlet *Revenge his foul and most unnatural murder* (line 31). If Hamlet obeys the Ghost he will condemn himself to the same purgatory that has just been described. The Ghost describes his murder as most *foul, strange and unnatural* (line 34). At least part of the hideousness of the murder was that it was committed against a king by a close relative: exactly what Hamlet is being asked to do.

The Ghost dwells on Gertrude's lust and sexual relations with her new husband—but tells Hamlet not to think badly of her. God will judge her. However, the Ghost has judged Claudius and wants Hamlet to be his instrument of revenge.

Given such a confusing series of messages, it is hardly surprising that Hamlet hesitates before committing himself to killing Claudius. This conversation between the living and the dead cunningly lays out all the dilemmas with which Hamlet has to wrestle. ✪ Do you think Hamlet has resolved them by the time he returns to Denmark in Act 5? How has he done this?

There is one other issue that could cause Hamlet to doubt the Ghost. Claudius never says how he murdered his brother. The idea of poisoning someone by pouring poison into their ear seems more a metaphor for someone being told lies than a practical way of killing anyone. Hamlet may feel poison is being poured into his own ears, that the Ghost is not his father's spirit at all but a shape-shifting demon bent on mischief.

Polonius: *a man faithful and honorable*

Polonius is the only representative (apart from the comic Osrick and the bit-parts of Voltemand and Cornelius) of the king's court. We see him offering advice to Claudius, but it is both verbose and, in the case of the cause of Hamlet's madness, completely wrong. We never see him more than loosely engaged in serious state matters.

We do see him running his family like a harsh and authoritarian court though. Polonius wants to control his children. Laertes evades control by being absent. Ophelia meekly gives way to her father's harsh instructions. He is shown to be neither affectionate nor pleasant. In fact there is an extremely sordid and unattractive streak that runs through everything Polonius does. He is also written as a comic

character, both in his own right—as a verbose, self-confusing speaker—and as a foil for Hamlet's wit. Shakespeare's combination of surface humor and an underlying sordidness creates a character that does more than fulfill a supporting role in the drama. Polonius is vital to many strands of the plot and it would have been too easy to have made him merely a collection of dramatic necessities.

It is his "nonrelationship" with his daughter that shows him at his most unpleasant. He never gives her a word of kindness. He accepts that Hamlet may have been attracted to her—indeed he may assume it too readily. But he never asks Ophelia what her feelings are towards Hamlet. In Act 1, scene 3, when she speaks of Hamlet her words can be interpreted as containing longing. This is the nearest she ever gets to daring to reveal her affection for the prince. But Polonius only sees his own position in this. Lines 114–118 are full of information about Polonius. He insults any capacity or right she may have for free thought by saying she should *Think yourself a baby.* He orders her to *Tender yourself more dearly*, not because she is worth it but because if she doesn't she'll tender him a fool.

❂ In Act 2, scene 2, line 190, Hamlet calls Polonius a fishmonger. This was Elizabethan slang for a pimp. What is the significance of this attack?

Polonius enjoys intrigue. He eavesdrops twice, the second time fatally. He uses an unnecessary and unpleasant subterfuge to find out about the behavior of Laertes in Paris. He uses his daughter as bait to find out the cause of Hamlet's madness.

It is difficult to assess Polonius's true feelings toward the royal family. He is of course deferential, even to Hamlet when he knows the Prince is making a fool of him. He appears to be ready to serve the king in any capacity. He is involved in the royal family's personal affairs far more deeply than his role as a court counselor requires. It is his interference in their private affairs that causes his death.

Polonius's verbosity creates several comic set pieces, notably his advice to Laertes (Act 1, scene 3, lines 60–87), his speech introducing the cause of Hamlet's madness (Act 2, scene 2, lines 104–116) and his description of the Players (Act 2, scene 2, lines 420–426). Apart from the comedy, these speeches provide striking contrast to Hamlet's expression of his thoughts in the long soliloquies. Polonius says much but means little: every line Hamlet speaks is full of meaning.

> ## Laertes: *a very noble youth*

In a play with such complex characters as Hamlet and Claudius, there simply isn't space nor dramatic need to have every other character written so fully. Laertes is crucial to the plot but he is more an attitude than a full character. He exists largely to provide a contrast to Hamlet. He is a far more simply written character. He might be one of the cast of a straightforward revenge tragedy who has wandered into a complex psychological drama.

This is not to say that Shakespeare's writing of Laertes is slipshod. Laertes's blunt, one-dimensional approach to life is a deliberate contrast to Hamlet's analysis and self-doubt. Look at Laertes's return to court in Act 4, scene 5. He thunders in demanding revenge for his father's death. In a few short and rather excessive exchanges with Claudius (in lines 126–175) he lays out his simple thirst for revenge. He doesn't even approach the moral questions and doubts that Hamlet has considered in his own revenge dilemma. Such an unthinking drive for revenge makes it easy for Claudius to manipulate Laertes.

Laertes has inherited two traits from his father: verbosity and an underlying unpleasantness. Whereas Polonius's verbal excesses were extended arguments, Laertes prefers the exaggerated rant. Within moments of arriving at Elsinore he is raging: *Vows to the blackest devil!/ Conscience and grace to the profoundest pit!* (Act 4, scene 5, lines 149–150). There may appear to be only a thin line between the tone of this outburst and some of Hamlet's more excessive utterances, but there is a world of difference in the content. Hamlet builds by logical analysis to a point of anger or frustration; Laertes bursts through the door already conjuring demons.

There is a strong whiff of theatricality about Laertes's outbursts. He is playing the blood-driven revenger perfectly. He appears unaware of the excesses of his language. But Hamlet is, and he mocks them in Act 5, scene 1. Laertes's grief seems overblown and hollow, and leaping into Ophelia's grave is just bad taste. His melodramatic manner would suit a simple revenge tragedy, but in *Hamlet* it makes him seem unthinking. Any gentler grief at Ophelia's death is pushed aside by his threats of vengeance:

> *O treble woe*
> *Fall ten times double on that cursed head*
> *Whose wicked deed thy most ingenious sense*
> *Deprived thee of!* (lines 258–261)

Hamlet's rant at Laertes shortly afterwards, beginning with the marvellous lines, *Woo't weep? Woo't fight? Woo't fast? Woo't tear thyself?/ Woo't drink up eisel? Eat a crocodile?* (lines 291–292) is not a return to his old madness but a cutting parody of Laertes's overblown rage.

So false does Laertes's grief sound that we might wonder if he is the sort of young man who is always looking for an excuse to start a fight. He does redeem himself at the very end when he appears to be sorry for what is happening to himself and Hamlet. And, crucially, he does point the accusing finger at Claudius.

Ophelia: *divided from herself*

Gertrude and Ophelia are the only women in the play. Given this, Ophelia's character is rather thin and passive. This is deliberate of course, but it raises the problem of why Hamlet should have been attracted to her, if indeed he ever really was. Perhaps she blossoms into a captivating and intelligent woman when freed from Polonius's scrutiny. There is, however, no evidence in the text to suggest this.

Ophelia expresses no point of view. Her only emotions are fear (after Hamlet's reported visit to her) or regret (at Hamlet's rejection of her). She never demands any freedom, nor questions Polonius's curt and misplaced instructions. She appears to have no understanding of Hamlet's madness, nor any curiosity as to its cause. Like Gertrude she has no soliloquy in which she can confide her true thoughts and feelings. (Maybe she doesn't have any!)

Compare her madness to Hamlet's and we find her passive nature still coming through. Hamlet's real or feigned madness results in combative attacks and sly battles of wits. Ophelia descends into a harmless, literally flowery witlessness. She is mad with grief, and resigns herself almost instantly to pretty nonsense.

✎ All this negativity is a shame because it diminishes the tragedy of her death and the pathos of her funeral. Of course we are moved to pity by the death of a young woman, and especially by Gertrude's extended lyrical account of the drowning. But that is an evocation of a tragic scene, not a report of a terrible waste of young vital life. We know too little about Ophelia to weep tears at her graveside.

❂ Do you think this is a fault in the structure of the play? Is *Hamlet* a play full of paradoxes? What other paradoxes are there in the plot and characterization?

The nature of Ophelia's death is interesting. Gertrude seems to suggest a tragic accident: suicide only because Ophelia did nothing to help herself once she had got into trouble. The coroner (*crowner,* Act 5, scene 1, line 4) has decided her death was accidental and that she can be buried in consecrated ground. But doubts remain: the First Gravedigger is skeptical. And the priest wants a short and hurried burial service because her death is *doubtful.*

❂ Actresses often find developing Ophelia's character difficult. Why? If you were directing an actress playing Ophelia, what would you suggest she do to make her into a more positive character, within the confines of the role?

Horatio: *more antique Roman than a Dane*

It is best to think of Horatio as standing slightly to one side of the drama of the play. He is there because he is Hamlet's friend; he has no deeper motive. His prime quality is trustworthiness, and his main purpose in the drama is to be Hamlet's ally. Without Horatio, Hamlet would need even more soliloquies to convey his thoughts and feelings. Horatio is a sort of one-man Greek chorus, keeping his calm while passions rage about him. It is no accident that the returned, rational Hamlet of Act 5 spends so much time in his company.

✎ By a few subtle comments from and about him, Horatio is established in the first scene as a man who is steady and trustworthy. We will believe what Horatio says. Like Hamlet, Horatio is brave, intelligent, and well educated. The reasons for their friendship are obvious. Horatio could be said to embody many of Hamlet's better qualities—qualities that Hamlet loses for a time in the unfolding drama. Horatio's virtues are always on view. He is the one thread of human goodness running through the play. His willingness to drink poison to follow his friend into death is a rare outburst of emotion. Hamlet does well to argue him out of this one rash outburst. Horatio will tell his friend's story very well.

Rosencrantz and Guildenstern:

those bearers put to sudden death

Say their names the other way around (Guildenstern first): the rhythm is unchanged. The king and queen swap their names in a light exchange of greetings (Act 2, scene 2, lines 35–36). This linguistic trick is deliberate: as characters Rosencrantz and Guildenstern are supposed to be interchangeable. They do not have separate identities. They never appear alone. They never disagree with one another. In productions they are often made indistinguishable to the rest of the characters to exploit their comic potential. Crucial to this is that they are not very bright.

In fact, as Shakespeare wrote them they are not stupid buffoons, but ordinary young men caught up in intrigues that are too big and complex for them. They lack the skills of cunning and dissembling in which others at court excel. They give away the cause of their visit almost instantly to Hamlet (Act 2, scene 2, lines 286–315).

Rosencrantz and Guildenstern are used in other people's plans: first by Claudius, then by Hamlet. We feel little sorrow at the report of their deaths. They have not acted as villains, but neither have they been true friends to Hamlet. They are shallow students caught in palace intrigues. We don't know why they choose to take part: we don't in fact know much about them at all. They don't appear to act with much free will, and leave their affairs to Fate, which is not kind to them. (Although the contemporary playwright Tom Stoppard did make them the "stars" of his play *Rosencrantz and Guildenstern Are Dead*, which tells some of the Hamlet story from their point of view.)

❷ Rosencrantz and Guildenstern's first conversation with Hamlet (Act 2, scene 2, lines 240–267) has an extended joke on the theme of Fate. What is the deeper significance of linking their appearance with Fate?

Osrick: *a waterfly*

Osrick (Osric in some texts) represents the court, doing the king's bidding after the death of Polonius. Like Polonius, Osrick over-uses and abuses language to comic effect. Beyond his ridiculous speech, an exaggerated pastiche of a style of discourse known as Euphuistic (see Commentary, p. 87), we don't learn much about this comic courtier. He provides the last flashes of humor before the dark climax of the play.

Perhaps the only serious note that Osrick sounds is that we can take the degeneration that clarity and meaning suffer in his words as symbolic of the corruption and chicanery of the court he represents.

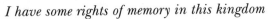

Fortinbras:

I have some rights of memory in this kingdom

Strictly speaking this is *young* Fortinbras, his dead father being *old* Fortinbras, King of Norway. There are parallels between Hamlet and Fortinbras. Both inherited their names from their fathers, but not their fathers' thrones, which in each case passed to uncles. Hamlet was born on the day his father killed Fortinbras's father in single combat. Old Hamlet became a war-like hero in the eyes of the world. Both fathers passed on warrior legacies to their sons.

Here the similarities end. Fortinbras is made in his father's mold. He tries to mount an expedition against Denmark to reclaim lands his father lost. He does this without the permission of his uncle, the current King of Norway. When stopped by Claudius's subtle intervention he is given an army and invited to go off and fight a pointless war with the Poles. Hamlet on the other hand has chosen to go to the university in Wittenberg. They never meet, though Hamlet witnesses Fortinbras's army crossing Denmark. If they had ever met they might not have had much to say to each other. There is a quiet tragedy in the fact that Fortinbras becomes King of Denmark: he may return the court to the ways of the older generation of war-like kings. The light of intellectualism that Hamlet and Horatio represented may well be snuffed out in Elsinore.

It is a cruel irony that Fortinbras should give Hamlet a soldier's funeral. He is trying to honor the son of his country's old enemy. He has gained the throne of Denmark by default but his first move is an act of misplaced kindness. Hamlet is nothing like his father: he would not want a soldier's funeral.

Test your knowledge

? Each of the characters discussed in this section is introduced with a quote from the text. Find where each quote comes from. Note what significance the quote has for the character.

Now you've searched the play for those quotes, take a break and let the book cool down.

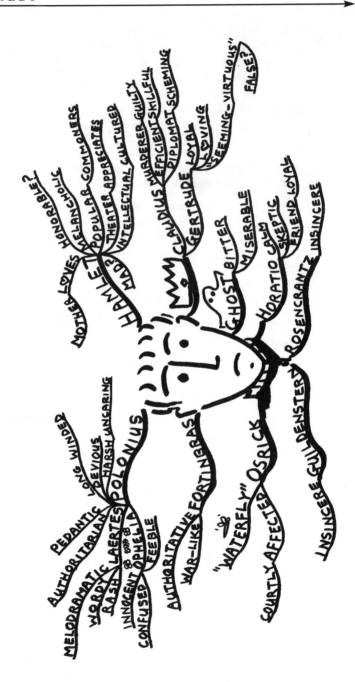

THEMES

THEATER

REVENGE

MORTALITY

WORDS & ACTIONS

CORRUPTION

MADNESS

Themes are the ideas explored by an author. They are the universal and broader messages of the story. They are not necessarily part of the mechanics of the plot. For example, Hamlet's meditation on death and the afterlife, expressed in great detail in his soliloquy in Act 3, scene 1 (lines 64–98), reveals a depth of analytical thinking that is necessary to the development of Hamlet's character. It shows us why Hamlet is hesitating to take revenge, and underlines the fact that Hamlet is a man of intellect not a creature of brute force or uncontrolled emotion. But Hamlet's long speech encompasses ideas that have long challenged thinking and belief in their own right. The ideas Shakespeare puts into Hamlet's mouth have resonance far beyond the limits of what is required of the character's role in the play. They are universal, philosophical ideas about belief—much more than just part of the plot.

Hamlet is a play with many themes. Revenge is the most important, being both the spring that drives the plot and the single element of the play that defines *Hamlet* as a revenge tragedy. Revenge and five other key themes are identified in the Commentary and Characterization sections of this guide with icons (see Key to icons, p. xiv).

Revenge

Hamlet is a revenge tragedy in the same way that *Romeo and Juliet* is a simple tale of thwarted lovers. Both plays have their roots in a particular style and form of drama but each goes far beyond what is typical of the genre. *Hamlet* has all the necessary ingredients of a revenge tragedy (see the notes on revenge tragedy in the Context section of this guide for a list, pp. 1–7), but brilliant characterization elevates *Hamlet* to the level of a masterpiece far beyond any other revenge tragedy.

To Shakespeare's audience revenge was an exciting and popular theme for drama. First performed in the period between Kyd's *The Spanish Tragedy* (1592) and Tourneur's *The Revenger's Tragedy* (1607), two landmarks of the genre, *Hamlet* told a type of story whose outline would have been familiar to Jacobean theater-goers.

It is important to know how common the notion of revenge was in Shakespeare's theater in order to understand why audiences knew that Hamlet had to act or face private torment. Today, few of us would feel compelled to "take the law into our own hands" to avenge a crime in the way that Hamlet feels he must. But the moral world that Hamlet inhabits, even if it is a fictional, theatrical one, demands that he does so.

It is not just Hamlet who is driven by revenge. Laertes is a far more typical revenge tragedy figure. He does not wrestle with his intellect or his conscience over whether or not to seek an eye for an eye. When he bursts back into the court in Act 4 he wants blood, plain and simple. Fortinbras also seeks revenge, though in a wider military and political world. He starts a campaign to regain lands for Norway that were taken by the man who killed his father in single combat.

Words and actions

More than in most other plays, characters in *Hamlet* hide their true feelings and motives behind their words. Hamlet feigns madness, Claudius maintains an air of calm and composure while racked with guilt, Rosencrantz and Guildenstern appear to be Hamlet's friends while rapidly becoming the king's agents. Often there is a conflict or contrast between the words characters speak and what they actually do or plot to do. They "act" in that they do not present their true selves.

This theme is explored in more detail in the Model Answer, pp. 104–109. But note that the exam question uses the terms "acting" and "actors" to mean this sort of dissembling by characters as well as referring to straightforward references to theater, which is treated in this section as a separate theme.

Madness

Pretending to be mad was a required stratagem of a revenge tragedy hero. But Hamlet's character is so complex, so revealed to the audience, that we share in his torments and indecisions. Sharing his anguish leads us to wonder if there is ever a point where he becomes genuinely mad. This possibility is dealt with at several points in the Commentary section, especially in the notes on Act 3, scene 4, and Act 4, scenes 1 and 2.

It is very hard to prove this either way. Hamlet's behavior and speech are the only indications, and of course we know that he intends (in Act 1, scene 5) to put on *an antic disposition*. Once in the role of a madman he only occasionally comes out and suggests to other characters that it might all be a charade. ❂ Find the places where he does this.

Too many of his *wild and whirling words* carry direct meaning for us to believe he's mad for any great length of time. In his "mad" exchanges with his enemies, Claudius, Polonius and Rosencrantz and Guildenstern, there is far too much "method in his madness." He is obviously playing with them. He may be testing them, to see how gullible they are. Polonius, the butt of so many sly attacks, never suspects that Hamlet is anything but crazy. The more intelligent and calculating Claudius on the other hand suspects throughout that Hamlet's madness is feigned. Remember, in all Hamlet's mad scenes there are in fact definite reasons for what he does and says.

Assessing Hamlet's true mental state is further complicated when we hear him apologizing to Laertes, apparently sincerely, for the wrongs he has suffered. Hamlet blames not himself but his madness. It sounds almost as if he is admitting that he fell foul of his own pretending and did actually do mad things: including killing Polonius and driving Ophelia to suicide.

There is no denying that Hamlet is prey to extreme fluctuations of mood, especially between intense introspection and sudden excitement. The depths of despair and sudden bursts of hatred he reveals in his soliloquies suggests a mind at best troubled and at worst teetering on the edge of reason. We do not know if Hamlet has always been like this or whether his father's death and mother's remarriage pushed him into mood swings between melancholia and anger.

Ophelia's madness is genuine and in stark contrast to Hamlet's. It is pathetic and tragic. She doesn't slip in and out of insanity. Her words have no connection with other characters. Though there are themes running through the remarks, snatches of song and rhymes she offers up in her two mad appearances, they merely suggest the causes of her madness. Ophelia has simply lost her perhaps always rather vague and simple mind.

Corruption

There are four main types of corruption in Hamlet: sexual corruption (the "incestuous" marriage of Claudius and Gertrude, corruption of Ophelia's purity suggested by Hamlet), moral corruption, bodily decay, and poison.

The first two are key elements in the plot. Hamlet appears driven to hate Claudius as much by his marriage to Gertrude as by the murder of his father. Moral corruption is linked to the idea of sex and sinning, but has other practical consequences in the play. Polonius's thinking that it is morally permissible to eavesdrop on private conversations causes his death. Rosencrantz and Guildenstern's visiting a friend but finding it easy to shift to acting as agent for his scheming stepfather is another morally questionable drift that ends fatally.

The idea of bodily decay is more a recurring theme of the imagery of the play than a dynamic in the plot. Shakespeare uses striking images of decay in almost every scene. Hamlet is given most of these images to heighten the power of his lines. His mother's remarriage *takes off the rose/ From the fair forehead of an innocent love/ And sets a blister there* (Act 3, scene 4, lines 51–53). Later in the same scene he describes Claudius as *a mildewed ear* (line 74).

Hamlet's talk of Polonius being eaten by worms in Act 4, scene 3, and his meditations over the skulls in the graveyard in Act 5, scene 1, are further graphic examples of his use of images of decay and bodily corruption.

The final type of corruption—poison and poisoning—is an ever-present source of death in the plot. Old Hamlet and Gertrude die by poisoning, plain and simple. Hamlet, Laertes, and Claudius all suffer wounds from a poisoned sword.

Something is rotten in the state of Denmark says Marcellus (Act 1, scene 4, line 100). Much of the rest of the play could be seen as Hamlet identifying and trying to put right what is wrong—corrupt—in the country.

Mortality

In *Hamlet,* eight characters meet violent ends, if we include Ophelia's *doubtful* death. That doesn't include Old Hamlet's murder, which is the spring that drives the revenge that is the heart of the play. Hamlet's first long speech (Act 1, scene 2, lines 133–164) tells us that he is so sick of life that he wishes it were not a sin to commit suicide. The contrast between life and death is constantly brought to the foreground by Hamlet's soliloquies, by the graveyard scene, and by the deaths that begin to occur with increasing rapidity as the play progresses. Notice that with Polonius's and Ophelia's deaths there is space after the event for other characters to meditate on their demise. This again gives occasion for life and death to be contrasted.

But the play does not dwell morbidly on death. There is a huge amount of humor in *Hamlet.* Death is simply a fact: however terrifying, it is inevitable. This may be the single most important thing that Hamlet has learned and which affects his actions and motives on his return to Elsinore in Act 5.

Theater

This is a more literal theme than the others. The icon identifies places in the play where theater and acting are discussed. All revenge tragedies featured a play within a play, and "The

Murder of Gonzago," or "The Mousetrap" as Hamlet suddenly decides to call it, is a vital part of the revenge plot in *Hamlet*. The title may sound strangely familiar. Crime writer Agatha Christie's murder mystery *The Mousetrap* is the longest-running play ever on the London stage (over forty years at the time of writing—summer 2000!).

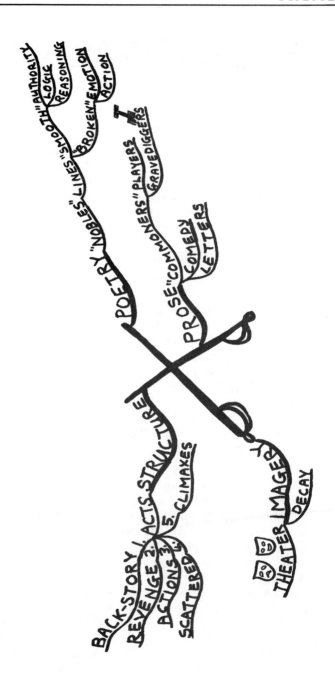

Poetry and prose

Most of *Hamlet* is written in blank verse. The basic line is an **iambic pentameter** of ten syllables divided into five pairs of unstressed/stressed syllables. It creates a regular pattern of sound, of alternating unstressed (soft) and stressed (hard) syllables, when read aloud. Try this with one of Hamlet's soliloquies. The rhythm gives a sense of grandeur and structure to the actor's lines. Don't forget that it is a play to be heard by an audience, not just studied on the page.

Unlike the "play within a play"—which is a pastiche of a simpler style of verse drama and has endless pairs of rhyming lines—there are few rhymes in the blank verse of *Hamlet*. There are pairs of rhyming couplets at the end of some scenes which are used to give a sense of closing. Hamlet's *O, what a rogue and peasant slave am I* soliloquy that ends Act 2, scene 2, concludes with the couplet *The play's the thing/ In which I'll catch the conscience of the King*. His soliloquy starting *How all occasions do inform against me* (Act 4, scene 4) has a final half-rhyming couplet: *O, from this time forth,/ My thoughts be bloody, or be nothing worth!* These rhymes also make good cues for actors and musicians waiting to start the next scene.

As in most of his plays, Shakespeare switches from poetry to prose to achieve certain dramatic effects. Few plays are written in verse today but for Elizabethans this was the most common type of language they heard on stage. They would have understood that prose was used for exchanges between servants, for comic scenes, and for reading letters. Broadly speaking, prose sounded less refined than poetry and so was usually given to "lower" characters: servants, clowns and madmen. But Hamlet switches between poetry and prose throughout. There are long exchanges in prose between Hamlet and the Players (Act 2, scene 2) and between Hamlet and the Gravedigger (Act 5, scene 1). They may lack the rhythmic and poetic force of blank verse, but these exchanges are as full of images and meaning as verse sections of the play.

Prose is also used extensively in *Hamlet's* comic and mad scenes. But notice that prose is used for one of his most profound and poetic speeches, as analytical and thought-packed as any of the soliloquies. This is the speech made to Rosencrantz and Guildenstern in Act 2, scene 2, lines 316–334. Shakespeare may have done this for variety. *Hamlet* has a greater range of writing styles than any of his other plays.

Switching between rhythmic blank verse and prose creates dramatic contrasts throughout the play. Look at Act 3, scene 1. Read aloud Hamlet's soliloquy and go on through his meeting with Ophelia. Notice how the calm, measured, introspective tone of the soliloquy is heightened by the blank verse in which it is written. Then, after a few broken, short exchanges, Hamlet's attack on Ophelia runs on in prose. Measured lines of verse would not accommodate his fury. It would sound too prepared. The contrast between the Hamlet of the soliloquy and the Hamlet ranting at Ophelia is reflected in the shift from poetry to prose.

Even with a considerable portion of *Hamlet* being in prose, Shakespeare was aware that endless lines of iambic pentameter can become sing-song. So he used a variety of devices to break up the pattern while still keeping a basic rhythm running. Shifts from the regular pattern usually link in with the meaning or emotional pitch of the speech and serve to heighten it. In speeches where something is being explained or recounted there will be "run-on" lines, where meaning runs over from one line to the next so seamlessly that there is no real break (when read aloud) between one line and the next. Claudius's smooth speeches in Act 1, scene 2, are good examples of this.

Speeches full of tortured emotion may have their lines broken up into two parts, which "added together" may have more than five stresses or ten syllables. Breaking the flow of the language in this way suggests a character struggling with intense feelings. Compare the calm and analytical *To be, or not to be* soliloquy (Act 3, scene 2) with the passionate, furious final third of the *O that this too too sullied flesh would melt* soliloquy (Act 1, scene 2). Notice the increased use of punctuation within lines and the repeating of words and phrases in this latter soliloquy.

Imagery

A major part of Shakespeare's genius is his use of images. He can invent sometimes very obscure and complex images but use them in such a way that they don't disturb the flow and pace of the drama. There is never a sense of the action slowing to allow a character to deliver a set piece filled with complex images and references. The poetry flows naturally through the drama of a scene, making us believe that these people Shakespeare has conjured up naturally speak in image-laden verse.

A Shakespeare play often has a recurring trend in its imagery which defines and sets the tone for much of the language. In *King Lear* references to storms, wild animals, and blindness occur in image after image. In *Hamlet,* one type of imagery dominates: corruption and decay. While corruption as a theme may not be as important as revenge or madness, as a source of imagery it is vital to the tone of the play.

Corruption, decay, rot, badness, madness: images reflecting these ideas are everywhere in *Hamlet.* The play is full of references to decay and corruption: physical and psychological, moral, and vegetable. Minds are diseased with *unwholesome* thoughts, the court and state are corrupted by bad actions, people die and become *pocky corses* fattened *for maggots.* How much of this obsession with decay is Hamlet's own morbid thoughts and view of his world, and how much is actually corrupt in the court and country is difficult to say. But disease and corruption are the overriding themes of the imagery throughout the play.

Just nine lines into the first scene of the play we learn that Francisco, a minor character, is *sick at heart.* His mood sets up an air of foreboding that will hang over the whole play. In the next scene, on the watch platform, Marcellus, another minor character, reminds us that *Something is rotten in the state of Denmark* (Act 1, scene 4, line 100). We begin to feel that Elsinore is an unhealthy place. Hamlet certainly thinks so. For him the decay is primarily moral and psychological. The decay set in with the death of his father and the accession of his uncle. Hamlet feels the world to be *an unweeded garden/ That grows to seed. Things rank and gross in nature/ Possess it merely* (Act 1, scene 2, lines 139–141).

Claudius and Laertes also reveal that decay and corruption are in their thoughts. Racked by guilt, Claudius compares Hamlet to a physical disease: *like the hectic in my blood he rages* (Act 4, scene 3, line 75). Laertes dwells on decay at Ophelia's funeral, *from her fair and unpolluted flesh/ May violets spring* (Act 5, scene 1, lines 249–250). And the Ghost's description of his murder is full of images of physical decay (Act 1, scene 5, lines 68–80).

Structure

Like Shakespeare's other great tragedies, *King Lear, Othello,* and *Macbeth*, the story of *Hamlet* unfolds over five Acts. It is Shakespeare's longest play. Acts 1 and 2 establish the scene and all main characters, and the revenge plot is set in motion. The first series of plot climaxes occur in Act 3. Then there are a number of short, scattered scenes in Act 4 before the threads of the plot draw together for two sets of dramatic climaxes in Act 5, first in the graveyard, then at the fencing match at court.

Decay on everyone's mind!

Identify the speaker in each of these quotes and say who or what is referred to.

1 *And a most instant tetter barked about,/ Most lazar-like, with vile and loathsome crust/ All my smooth body.*
2 *For if the sun breed maggots in a dead dog ...*
3 *And yet to me what is this quintessence of dust?*
4 *O, my offence is rank. It smells to heaven.*
5 *Nay, but to live/ In the rank sweat of an enseamed bed.*
6 *It will but skin and film the ulcerous place/ While rank corruption, mining all within/ Infects unseen.*
7 *Diseases desperate grown/ By desperate appliances are relieved.*
8 *A certain convocation of politic worms are e'en at him.*
9 *She may strew/ Dangerous conjectures in ill-breeding minds.*
10 *We have many pocky corses nowadays that will scarce hold the laying in.*

(Answers, see p. 91)

Take a break before the commentary.

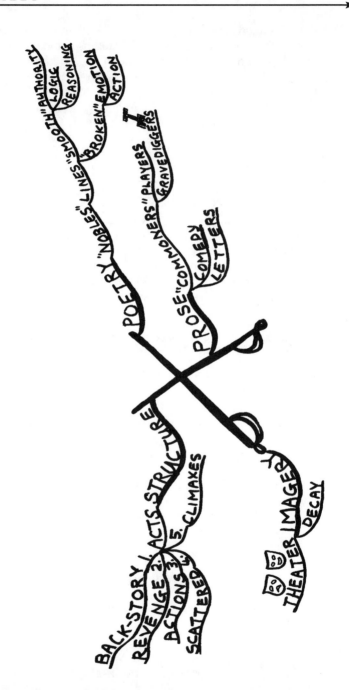

OMMENTARY

Act 1, scene 1

◆ The Ghost appears to soldiers keeping watch on the gun platform of Elsinore Castle, and to Horatio who challenges it.

This scene contains quite a lot of indirect **exposition** (conveying the background to events that take place in the play). Exchanges between characters neatly set up the political background and mood in Denmark and at the court. It is also full of action and drama.

Francisco is *sick at heart* (line 9), either because of his lonely watch on the battlements or because of wider issues troubling him about Denmark. He is relieved by Barnardo (who in some texts is called "Bernardo"). As Francisco is leaving he meets Horatio and Marcellus on their way to join Barnardo. We learn that the Ghost has appeared twice before at the dead of night, and that Horatio, a scholar, has been invited along to give his opinion of the apparition. He is established as a skeptic by Marcellus's comment:

Horatio says 'tis but our fantasy,
And will not let belief take hold of him. (lines 28–29)

The Ghost appears. It bears a striking resemblance to the recently dead king, Old Hamlet. Horatio, perhaps bolder than the rest because of his skepticism, challenges it to speak. But he offends the Ghost by suggesting that it usurps the appearance of the old king as he looked when dressed in armor for battle. The Ghost stalks away. Horatio is shocked: it seems he has lost some of his skepticism. He takes the Ghost's appearance as a bad omen for Denmark.

Horatio and Marcellus provide more background information about political events in Denmark and at court. There are preparations for a possible war with Norway:

So nightly toils the subject of the land,
And why such daily cast of brazen cannon
And foreign mart for implements of war. (lines 83–85)

Suddenly the Ghost returns. Horatio speaks more gently to it this time. He asks it if it can speak, if it needs anything done to ease its troubled spirit. Just as the Ghost appears to be ready to speak, the cock crows and it vanishes.

As dawn breaks Horatio's skepticism returns. When Marcellus talks of how at Christmas time no ghosts dare walk abroad because of the holiness of the season Horatio replies *So I have heard and do in part believe it* (line 180). It might be that he now partly believes this superstition because of what he has just seen. Despite this grudging acceptance of the supernatural, Horatio needs to be a voice of rationality and reason throughout the play to counter the darker, more primitive forces that gather around his friend Hamlet.

The men decide to tell Hamlet what they have seen. So far they have not mentioned anything about the Prince, what he may be feeling about the possible war, and the atmosphere of foreboding that seems to be hanging over the court. This creates suspense as we await the arrival on stage of the eponymous Prince of Denmark.

Look at the language of this scene. Long passages of exposition (Marcellus, lines 81–90, Horatio, lines 91–119) are written in flowing iambic pentameter, while many of the action-related exchanges, especially when the Ghost appears, are in chopped, shorter lines. ❂ What dramatic effect do these contrasting styles of writing create?

Barnardo, Francisco, and Marcellus are all minor characters who only appear in the first Act. Their names are rather confusing for a drama set in Denmark: Marcellus is Latinate, suggesting classical drama, while Barnardo and Francisco are Spanish names. Their military rank and role at court is not made clear. But they are jointly referred to (by Horatio, Act 1, scene 2, lines 203 and 206) as *gentlemen,* so they are clearly more than humble guardsmen. Horatio is important in that he becomes Hamlet's one true confidant and finally the keeper of his reputation, but he has no personal stake in the main drama.

Act 1, scene 2

◆ Claudius, the new Danish king, addresses his court. He tells of his marriage to Gertrude, Old Hamlet's widow, and sends ambassadors to negotiate with Norway and prevent war.

◆ Claudius and Gertrude urge Hamlet to stop mourning his father. Hamlet is at odds with the court. In a soliloquy he expresses his disgust with the world.

◆ Horatio, Marcellus, and Barnardo tell Hamlet about the Ghost. Hamlet is determined to join the watch that night and speak to it.

Like scene 1, this is packed with information setting up the state of the court and, more importantly, the relationships between Hamlet, Claudius and Gertrude. On stage, the arrival of the court in full splendor (the first stage direction is *flourish*) provides a sudden upbeat spectacle after the gloom of the previous scene. We move from dark into light, but Hamlet's two soliloquies quickly let us know that there may be darker things than a wandering spirit festering under the veneer of court splendor.

Claudius opens the scene with two long speeches totalling fifty lines, interrupted only by a one-line farewell from Voltemand and Cornelius. He is usually portrayed on stage as a smooth and confident operator, verbally skillful, and in command of his court. His language echoes this: lines flow on neatly from one to another and the iambic pentameter rhythm is consistent.

He neatly balances the sorrow he and the court felt at the death of the old king with the joy he (and they, presumably) feel at his accession and marriage to his dead brother's widow. But his fluent and reasoned account of what has happened would have jarred with an Elizabethan audience: they would have regarded his marriage to Gertrude as incestuous. However, Gertrude stands steadfastly (and usually on stage happily) beside her new husband.

Claudius moves seamlessly on to describe how he proposes to avert war with Norway by negotiation. Voltemand and Cornelius are despatched as envoys. Claudius is a king whose authority is based on diplomacy, in contrast to the warlike figure of Old Hamlet. He appears relaxed and in command, but there are hints of steely authority beneath the polished surface: he warns his ambassadors not to take one step beyond the terms he has laid out in his letter to Norway.

✪ Read Claudius's two opening speeches carefully. How do you think relations stand between him and the court? What hints are you given?

When Claudius asks Hamlet to cease mourning his father, his smooth authority grinds to a halt. He calls Hamlet *my son* (line 67): Hamlet reacts with the cutting aside *A little more than kin, and less than kind*! Gertrude loyally supports her new husband and in gentle terms urges Hamlet to be less downcast. He replies stingingly. Claudius turns from sympathizing with Hamlet to criticizing his continued mourning in a long speech (lines 90–121) which culminates in him refusing Hamlet permission to return to the university in Wittenberg. Gertrude neatly turns this into a request and Hamlet, equally neatly, says *I shall in all my best obey you, madam* (line 124): note the "you". The king sees this as a cause for celebratory drinking in the coming evening, underlining a tendency toward drunken excess that we have already heard is rife in his court.

There is a feeling under the surface that everyone suspects everyone else of acting. Gertrude thinks Hamlet is affecting excessive grief, while Hamlet thinks she must have been only acting the sorrowful widow such a short time before. We will come to see that disguising one's true nature is part of the way Claudius's court operates.

Left alone, Hamlet expresses his disgust with the new king and with the actions of his mother. He speaks of his father with exaggerated admiration. He recalls him not as a man but as a superhero, who protected and enthralled his adoring queen. But Hamlet's despair goes much wider than familial circumstances: his whole view of life is tainted with a melancholy verging on loathing. The world is *stale, flat, and unprofitable* (line 137), *an unweeded garden/ That grows to seed* (lines 139–140). He wishes that suicide were not a mortal sin. He claims his father has been dead only a few weeks, while Gertrude and Claudius gave the impression that a longer period of time had elapsed and that it is now appropriate for mourning to end.

Notice the amount of punctuation in this soliloquy and compare it to the more flowing lines of Claudius's long speeches. Hamlet's lines are often broken into shorter, disjointed utterances, creating the effect of someone struggling with his emotions.

Horatio, Marcellus, and Barnardo arrive and tell Hamlet about the Ghost. We learn that Horatio is a fellow student at Wittenberg and a good friend of Hamlet's. The connection

between Hamlet and the others is unclear but they again
appear to be more than just professional soldiers on castle
duties. Given that Hamlet comes to appear such a solitary
character at the court, locked in his quest for revenge, it is
worth noting that here he appears to have loyal and robust
friends around him.

Left alone for a second time, Hamlet tells us that the
appearance of his father's spirit makes him suspect that
foul play was involved in his death.

Act 1, scene 3

◆ Laertes warns Ophelia not to accept demonstrations of love
  from Hamlet.
◆ Polonius offers his advice on life to Laertes, then warns
  Ophelia to reject Hamlet. She agrees.

Polonius and his two children are introduced. What happens to
them forms the subplot of the play, but it is dependent upon
the main drama. Everything that befalls them originates from
Hamlet's actions.

Laertes warns Ophelia that Hamlet's desires will alter as
he grows older. He is a prince and may not be allowed
to choose who to love as freely as other men can. Laertes's
warnings seem to be tinged with excessive caution, and even
prudery; especially when he says *The chariest maid is prodigal
enough/ If she unmask her beauty to the moon* (lines 40–41).
This is a very puritanical view for a young man. His advice
runs to 35 lines; Ophelia replies in just seven. She does not
challenge anything he says. She does nothing to suggest that
she might find rejecting Hamlet painful.

Polonius interrupts them, delaying Laertes with 27 lines of
advice and *precepts*. His is much more wide-ranging advice,
covering everything from how to dress to personal finances.
Although there is actual good sense in what he says, actors
usually play this speech for comic effect, with Laertes eager to
go and Polonius's list seemingly endless. A good interpretation
should establish Polonius as a man who loves the sound of his
own voice and never uses one word if five will do.

As soon as Laertes is gone Polonius asks Ophelia what advice
Laertes gave her. Polonius orders her to break off all contact

with Hamlet. He is surprisingly critical of Hamlet, who is a prince and set over him in the court hierarchy:

> *Do not believe his vows. For they are*
> *... mere implorators of unholy suits,*
> *Breathing like sanctified and pious bawds*
> *The better to beguile.* (lines 136–140)

Polonius may share Laertes's covert puritanism, and he is probably ready to criticize Hamlet (out of his earshot) by assuming that his years carry wisdom and authority over Hamlet's youth. Once again, in reply to a lengthy and powerful speech directed at instructing her, Ophelia meekly and briefly agrees to obey.

Compare how Polonius speaks to each of his children. He is indulgent and practical towards Laertes. The scene is often played as though Polonius knows that "young men will be young men" but he'll offer the advice anyway knowing it will be ignored. But with Ophelia he reveals a far harsher, more unpleasant side. He seems to assume that Ophelia is naturally weak (because of her sex?) and ready to give in to her own passions or Hamlet's advances. He is not prepared to offer her freedom to express her own wishes. He advises Laertes; he orders Ophelia.

Laertes is very much made in his father's mold. There is a parallel between the lengthy advice he gives Ophelia and the list of *precepts* that he is given by Polonius. Laertes's words to his sister are solidly worked out, middle-aged in tone and untouched by any youthful affection or humor. Polonius's advice to his son reads like a speech a principal might give at a school assembly.

Act 1, scenes 4 and 5

◆ Hamlet, Horatio, and Marcellus watch for the Ghost. It appears and Hamlet follows it alone to a farther part of the castle.

◆ The Ghost reveals his identity, and how he met his death. He urges Hamlet to seek revenge.

◆ Hamlet is joined by Horatio and Marcellus. He makes them swear to keep silent about what they have seen. He warns them that he might need to pretend some sort of madness, but they must never suggest that it is feigned.

All that separates these scenes is a brief interlude when the Ghost leads Hamlet away from Horatio and Marcellus to speak privately. It is best read (and on stage is nearly always performed) as one long scene with six main events: the wait on the gun platform; the Ghost's appearance and Hamlet's running after it; the Ghost's conversation with Hamlet; Hamlet's vowing revenge; Horatio and Marcellus swearing their oath; and Hamlet's hinting at future feigned madness.

As they wait on the gun platform Hamlet, Horatio and Marcellus hear cannon the court set off when they are drinking toasts. It is a Danish custom but Hamlet complains that it gives the Danes a bad reputation among other countries. There is a feeling that these three men, watching on the castle roof while the revels go on below, stand outside the court that they feel extends no warmth toward them.

The Ghost appears and beckons Hamlet to follow it. Horatio and Marcellus try to prevent him. Horatio, previously the skeptic, now seems to have a great knowledge of ghosts, warning Hamlet that the Ghost may well lead him to the top of the nearby cliff *And there assume some other horrible form ... And draw you into madness* (scene 4, lines 81, 83). But Hamlet will not be stopped. He runs off, following the Ghost. Horatio and Marcellus decide to follow, but they take some time to find him. Meanwhile, the Ghost and Hamlet speak.

The Ghost confirms that he is the spirit of Hamlet's father. He must walk the nights and burn in purgatorial fires during the day *Till the foul crimes done in my days of nature/ Are burnt and purged away* (scene 5, lines 17–18). He describes how Claudius murdered him while he slept in his orchard. There is no indication from the Ghost as to whether Gertrude had already been seduced by Claudius, who then killed him as a rival in love. The Ghost continues the Christian theme begun by his description of purgatory by saying that it was dreadful to be murdered without a chance to confess or pray. He died in the *blossoms of my sin...sent to my account/ With all my imperfections on my head* (lines 83, 85–86). ✪ Have we had any other specific Christian references so far in the play?

This is the second time the Ghost has referred in graphic terms to the sins he committed while alive. Even for an age where most people believed in Original Sin (it was assumed that children were born sinful, and were therefore sinners before even doing anything wrong!), the Ghost paints a very black view of his life, which sits at odds with Hamlet's memory of his father's perfection.

The Ghost says that Hamlet's revenge will cleanse the royal bed which is now *A couch for luxury and damned incest* (line 90). Hamlet has already referred to the *incestuous sheets* of Claudius's and Gertrude's marriage bed (Act 1, scene 2, line 162). These intimate details focus uncomfortably on the very physical nature of the crime the Ghost sees has been committed by Claudius and Gertrude in marrying. But the Ghost orders Hamlet not to harm or condemn Gertrude: she must be left to face God's judgment (a further religious reference) and her own conscience. As dawn approaches, the Ghost flees.

The Ghost has given Hamlet a number of double messages. He says *Pity me not* (line 9), then goes on to detail some of the horrors of his purgatory that can only summon up pity in his son. He speaks luridly of Gertrude's sexual depravity, but orders his son not to think badly of her. Most perplexing for Hamlet is that the Ghost is asking him to commit an act that will inevitably condemn him to suffer the same purgatory after death that the Ghost has described in such awful terms. The Ghost says that his death at the hands of his brother was a *foul and most unnatural murder* (line 31). Yet he is asking Hamlet to commit the same kind of crime: the murder of a close family member (an uncle) and a king. Hamlet is caught between two options: saving himself from purgatory and breaking the code that the Ghost holds that blood must be revenged by blood; or condemning himself by upholding and acting upon the command to commit murder.

However much Hamlet's later indecision and delay might be caused by these dilemmas, his next soliloquy (lines 99–119) is an explosion of anger and sworn vengeance. Notice that the first six lines are each broken by punctuation into two or more short exclamations. Hamlet is a man transformed, so much so that one feels the Ghost's words have simply confirmed what Hamlet has already suspected. They have enlarged to fury the dull hatred and melancholy he already felt.

When Horatio and Marcellus catch up with Hamlet they find his words *wild and whirling* (line 148). His evasions when they ask him what has happened are already tinged with the linguistic tricks he uses later to suggest madness. ✪ Do you think some of his madness is real? What could have caused or contributed to it?

Hamlet finally tells them that the Ghost is *honest* (line 154). Horatio's skeptical intellectualism is referred to again when Hamlet says *There are more things in heaven and earth, Horatio,/ Than are dreamt of in your philosophy* (lines 187–188). He does not reveal what the Ghost has told him but swears them to secrecy about what they have witnessed.

Hamlet then tells them that he may in the future act as if he is mad but they must always remember that this is a ruse designed to help him on a course of action to achieve a purpose that he does not explain to them. This must be a most perplexing warning.

The classic plot of a revenge tragedy has been set in motion. There is now an inevitability in what Hamlet will have to do. Elizabethan audiences, used to seeing such tragedies on stage, would have identified the personal foreboding and doom in Hamlet's heartfelt complaint *The time is out of joint. O cursed spite,/ That ever I was born to set it right* (lines 210–211). Hamlet recognizes the role that has been cast for him. Even though his hatred for Claudius is genuine, it is a cruel twist of fate that he should find himself the revenger in a revenge tragedy.

Know your court

? Make a Mind Map of all the figures in the court at Elsinore, except Hamlet, and beside each one put a single word which you think most effectively sums up his or her character so far.

Test your knowledge

Beside each of these quotes from Act 1 put (a) the name of the speaker, (b) who he or she is speaking to or about.

1 *Let us once again assail your ears,/ That are so fortified against our story/ What we have two nights seen.*

2 *If thou hast any sound or use of voice,/ Speak to me.*

3 *You cannot speak of reason to the Dane/ And lose your voice. What wouldst thou beg ...*

4 *I shall in all my best obey you madam.*

5 *Affection? Pooh! You speak like a green girl.*

6 *If thou hast nature in thee, bear it not./ Let not the royal bed of Denmark be/ A couch for luxury.*

7 *O most pernicious woman!*

8 *O villain, villain, smiling, damned villain!*

9 *Well said old mole! Canst work i'th'earth so fast?*

10 *And still your fingers on your lips, I pray.*

(Answers, see p. 91)

*Feel like you've just seen a ghost?
Take a break.*

Act 2, scene 1

◆ Polonius sends Reynaldo to spy on Laertes in Paris.

◆ Ophelia recounts the strange visit she has been paid by Hamlet. Polonius decides to tell Claudius about it.

Reynaldo's mission is partly a device to let us know that some time has elapsed since the last scene: time in which Hamlet has apparently been demonstrating signs of madness. If Laertes needs money, he must have been away for a while. He does not seem the wild and excessive type. There is a definite strain of unpleasantness in Polonius throughout this scene. He appears to be hoping that Reynaldo (the name hints at Reynard, the nickname for a fox) will find Laertes breaking some of the precepts he offered in Act 1, scene 3. Polonius can be played with fatherly kindness and concern, but actors usually suggest Polonius is the sort of old man who likes his worst fears confirmed. It creates a comic element in his character.

Polonius wants Reynaldo to put about a few slanders concerning Laertes. Polonius is quick to suggest ideas: that his son visits brothels, gets drunk, etc. Friends will either confirm that Laertes is the sort of man to do these things, or show surprise because they feel he is too respectable to have such faults. Reynaldo will then know how Laertes is behaving without having to ask direct questions. That Polonius, chief and respected statesman at Claudius's court, conducts his family affairs in this devious manner suggests he is also a scheming counselor. But perhaps scheming is appropriate in the court where Claudius presides. ✪ What do you think?

Shakespeare lightens the tone by giving Polonius a comic side too. He is so in love with his own words in this scene that he frequently forgets the point of his argument.

✪ Read the scene carefully up to the point where Ophelia enters. If you were directing the scene for stage would you portray Polonius in a comic way or as a sour old man? Find quotations to support your interpretation.

Ophelia enters and gives a graphic account of the frightening visit she has just had from a clearly deranged Hamlet. Polonius takes very little interest in his daughter's distress. He immediately sees the information as material to be passed to the king and used in the now public matter of finding out the cause of Hamlet's madness.

Several weeks have passed since the meeting between the Ghost and Hamlet, so it is not this event that has prompted Hamlet's distraction. Polonius sees another cause: Ophelia has obeyed her father and rebuffed any advances from Hamlet, and this has driven him mad with unrequited love.

Given that Hamlet has not even uttered Ophelia's name, it seems unlikely that he is obsessed with love for her and has just forgotten to mention this to anyone or share it with the audience via a soliloquy. Much more likely is that his visit was part of his feigned madness. If so, it is a cruel use of Ophelia. But there are sound practical, if heartless, reasons why he would choose the naïve and impressionable girl for a display of his *antic disposition*. He knows she will immediately tell Polonius, and he will tell the king.

Read Ophelia's speech describing Hamlet's frightening visit carefully. The rhythm and structure of the blank verse are perfect. The lines flow smoothly. Compare this to Hamlet's fragmented and emotionally charged response to the appearance of the Ghost in the previous scene (lines 99–119). Ophelia seems very composed for an innocent girl who has just been visited by a madman.

Act 2, scene 2

◆ Rosencrantz and Guildenstern arrive.
◆ Ambassadors from Norway return.
◆ Polonius convinces Claudius and Gertrude that unrequited love for Ophelia has made Hamlet mad.
◆ The "mad Hamlet" makes his first appearance and spars verbally with Polonius.
◆ Hamlet makes Rosencrantz and Guildenstern confess that they were *sent for*.
◆ The Players arrive. At Hamlet's request, the First Player recites a speech and reduces himself to tears.
◆ Left alone, Hamlet muses on his failure to avenge his father's murder, comparing himself with the actor who moved himself to tears reciting a fictional tale.

This enormous scene of over 600 lines is best studied as seven separate sections, based on the events listed above.

(1) Claudius is troubled by Hamlet's apparent descent into madness and has summoned Rosencrantz and Guildenstern, two of Hamlet's former school friends. His intentions are ambiguous. He genuinely wants them to find out the cause of Hamlet's madness, but whether this is so that Hamlet's mental suffering can be cured, or whether Claudius already suspects Hamlet's state has something to do with his own crimes, is not clear. Careful reading soon establishes that the king is thinking of himself, not Hamlet. He is keen to let Rosencrantz and Guildenstern know that they will be paid: *Your visitation shall receive such thanks/ As fits a king's remembrance* (lines 25–26). Claudius is ensuring that if it comes to a matter of sides, Rosencrantz and Guildenstern will be on his. ❍ What do you think Gertrude hopes will be achieved by their visit?

(2) Polonius announces the return of the ambassadors sent to Norway. The news is good: Fortinbras is now being paid to mount an expedition against the Poles. He wants permission for his troops to cross Danish land. The successful outcome of these negotiations shows the positive qualities of Claudius's leadership. This prevents him from declining into a purely villainous figure too rapidly. His wisdom has served his country well: he has gained what he required from Norway

without recourse to the combat that Old Hamlet would no doubt have chosen. The news that Fortinbras will be about on the edges of events prepares us for his appearance at the end of the play.

(3) Polonius guides events from the political to the private when the ambassadors exit, announcing self-importantly that he has found the cause of Hamlet's madness. His comic, wordy explanations (lines 92–121) test the patience of the king and queen. He fails to heed his own dictum, *brevity is the soul of wit* (line 97). ✪ What dramatic effect does this comic element serve within this long, event-packed scene?

Eventually (lines 140–160) he convinces the king and queen that Ophelia's refusal to respond to Hamlet's overtures of love has driven Hamlet:

> *Thence to a watch, thence into a weakness,*
> *Thence to a lightness, and, by this declension,*
> *Into the madness where he now raves.* (lines 157–159)

Claudius is eager to test Polonius's theory and agrees to have Ophelia loiter where they know Hamlet will pass by. Polonius and the king will eavesdrop on their conversation. Once again Polonius is shown as scheming; choosing an indirect route to achieve his ends. They could try just asking Hamlet about his feelings toward Ophelia! Once again meek Ophelia is being controlled by someone else.

✪ Polonius defers to Claudius and Gertrude because he is their subject, but what other reasons might he have for trying to impress them with his knowledge and devotion at this time?

(4) Hamlet enters. This is the first time we have seen him in the role of madman. Polonius wants to be left alone with Hamlet, and urges Claudius and Gertrude to permit this. There is a lengthy series of comic exchanges in which Hamlet entirely gets the better of Polonius. There is wit in exchanges such as,

> POLONIUS: *Will you walk out of the air my lord?*
> HAMLET: *Into my grave?* (lines 224–225)

At the same time, bitter satire is always present in Hamlet's lines in this scene. It is easy to read Hamlet's words not as those of a madman but of a prince disgusted by the scheming of the court, and of Polonius especially, and using his rank to vent his anger. Note how deferential Polonius is to Hamlet at all times. The bitterness Hamlet feels for life wells up at the end of the exchange (lines 224–225) when he again mentions his desire to cease living.

(5) Hamlet seems briefly and genuinely lifted out of his bitterness by the arrival of Rosencrantz and Guildenstern. They exchange clever banter which shows them to be old friends and reveals Hamlet's now little-practiced intellectual wit. But his mood gradually darkens as he becomes aware that his friends are at Elsinore only because they were sent for. Realizing this, Hamlet quickly realigns his position. While still maintaining an apparent air of friendship, he forces them to confess that they were summoned by Claudius and Gertrude.

After they have confessed, Hamlet appears both more guarded and more respectful of them, perhaps acknowledging their honesty at least. Hamlet explains his melancholy in a long and image-packed speech (lines 316–334). It is another example of Shakespeare using Hamlet to voice ideas that extend beyond what is necessary to flesh out his role. Hamlet's speech is an all-embracing view of the hollowness of life. It shows Hamlet's intellectual energy, his imagination, and the depth of his despair.

Notice how Shakespeare turns the end of the speech back into a conversation between friends by a clever little sexual joke. If the lofty philosophical tone had been maintained throughout, Hamlet would have been left stranded on a pinnacle of fine words and intellectual musings. The exchange between him and Rosencrantz (lines 335–350) brings the tone "back to earth" and moves us toward the arrival of the players. It is an example of bathos: a sudden, usually comic, descent from a high philosophical or intellectual pitch to the commonplace.

The conversation that Rosencrantz and Hamlet have between this point and the arrival of the Players (lines 335–391) is a diversion from the plot: a discussion about theater and about particular events that would have been common knowledge to Shakespeare's audience. It was probably included to add a popular dimension to the play. The only plot development it provides is to show how keenly Hamlet is interested in theater. It deals with issues that have nothing to do with Denmark in the Dark Ages, but with the London theater in Shakespeare's time.

The Players Rosencrantz and Guildenstern passed on their way to court are *tragedians of the city* who have been forced to tour because of custom lost to companies of child actors, the *little eyases* of line 364. This is a thinly veiled reference to the 1601 War of the Theatres in London, which exploded out of rivalry between companies of (adult) actors and theaters where children's troupes performed. There was much insult thrown about between the theaters, and the boys' companies became feared for the vicious satire against other theaters that was written into their performances. (After a few months the boys drifted out of fashion and people returned to adult performances.)

This now rather obscure sidetrack is brought to a sudden halt by the key lines Hamlet suddenly delivers to Guildenstern:

I am but mad north-north-west. When the wind is southerly, I know a hawk from a handsaw. (lines 402–403)

Of course, many madmen will say that they are not mad, but it is more likely that Hamlet is playing with his old friends. He has seen through them, assessed them and knows they are no match for him. They are out of their depth in the intrigues of the court. But if he is keeping to the plan he alluded to with Horatio and Marcellus, then he is telling them the truth.

(6) Hamlet is excited and pleased by the arrival of the Players. New life is injected into this long scene. Directors often make the Players seem larger than life, with vibrant costumes to contrast with Hamlet's mourning and the court's formal clothes. As actors (with Hamlet's enthusiastic support), they stand a little outside of court conventions and hierarchy. Though they are ultimately the king's subjects, they are free men and women who come and go and are not bound by court careers.

Polonius's reappearance bearing the now stale news of their arrival is another chance for Hamlet to engage in cutting exchanges with the old courtier. This time Polonius's side of the exchange is almost entirely comic: his verbose description of the actors (lines 420–426) is pure word-play. Notice though that Polonius, a staid and sober figure so far, concerned only with court business and the correct conduct of his children, is excited about the arrival of the Players. Shakespeare has created a court where theater is valued and enjoyed.

Hamlet is much more calculating in his exchanges than the others think: he throws out another hook to catch Polonius when he alludes to *Jephthah, judge of Israel* (lines 427–434). It is calculated to convince Polonius that unrequited love is the true source of his madness. We have to listen closely to Hamlet: in the midst of comic banter and apparent asides he slips in lines of absolute honesty regarding his true condition. ✪ Does Hamlet actually lie about himself at any point in this scene?

Hamlet further reveals his knowledge of theater when he asks the First Player to recite, as *a taste of your quality … a passionate speech* (lines 455–456). Hamlet can recall the speech and gives a skillful recitation of the opening lines. He is clearly a keen supporter of theater, perhaps with an actor's skills. The comparison between this and his feigned madness is obvious. We are reminded that theater, and role-playing, are key elements of the plot.

The First Player takes up the speech Hamlet began. It is part of a classical tale of the Trojan Wars. Despite interruptions from

Polonius, the actor moves himself to tears. He finishes and there is a bitter exchange between Polonius and Hamlet. Shakespeare weaves in yet another reference to theater when he warns Polonius to ensure the Players are well accommodated, saying (of actors generally): *they are the abstract and brief chronicles of the time. After your death you were better to have a bad epitaph than their ill report while you live* (lines 550–553)—a warning from the stage to any in the audience who might have denigrated actors!

Hamlet privately requests that the Players present *The Murder of Gonzago* for the court on the next evening. Mysteriously, Hamlet requests the First Player to learn an extra speech that he will write to go into the play. This creates a dramatic expectation towards the scene's close.

(7) Alone on stage, Hamlet delivers another great and lengthy soliloquy (lines 576–634). As with most of his soliloquies and other long meditative speeches, he ranges far beyond his starting point—his own position and emotions—into wider philosophical realms. He has been shaken by the ability of the First Player to move himself to tears of passion for the suffering of Hecuba, a character from a Greek myth (*What's Hecuba to him, or he to her*, line 586), while he, Hamlet, is unable to rouse himself to sufficient passion to avenge his own father's murder.

He expresses his shame at his own inadequacies: *O, what a rogue and peasant slave am I* (line 577). The soliloquy has a definite progression. He moves from expressing his self-disgust to explaining how he will use the play the following evening as a way of testing the guilt of Claudius. It depicts a murder identical to the one the Ghost said was perpetrated upon him.

Hamlet adds another thread to this magnificent speech. From line 586 on he falls back into doubt, wondering whether the Ghost really is the spirit of his father. It *May be a devil, and the devil hath power/ T'assume a pleasing shape* (lines 627–629). He feels he could fall prey to such deception because of *my weakness and my melancholy* (line 630), a confession that his mental state, though probably far from madness, is disturbed or deeply depressed. Given that much of this scene has been devoted to suggestions and demonstrations of feigned madness, this adds a complex spin to his state of mind, and to this darkening revenge tragedy.

Test yourself

? Draw a Mind Map identifying all the ways in which theater is used or referred to in Act 2, scene 2.

? Imagine you overheard Hamlet's long soliloquy that ends Act 2. List his main points in your own words.

Test your knowledge

1 What five vices does Polonius say Reynaldo may claim Laertes indulges in?
2 What was wrong with the way Hamlet was dressed when he visited Ophelia?
3 What specific act of Ophelia's does Polonius think has driven Hamlet mad?
4 What news is to be the *fruit to that great feast*?
5 What does Hamlet say he reads, and what is the matter?
6 What does Hamlet describe as a *quintessence of dust*?
7 What was the treasure that Jephthah had?
8 Who praises Hamlet's speaking of the first part of the *passionate speech*?
9 Who does Polonius want to use *according to their desert*?
10 Who can *assume a pleasing shape*?

(Answers, see p. 92)

Hamlet talks to himself—take a break before you start doing the same.

Act 3—Overview

Events follow one another quickly throughout this Act, which takes place in a single day. Characters prowl around the castle following their own plans and deceptions. Things are beginning to shift toward crisis. Claudius's confession at prayer in scene 3 symbolizes the cracking of the smooth veneer of the court generally. Many Shakespeare plays have an intense and action-packed third Act. It is structurally the right point in a five-Act play to have the first dramatic climaxes.

Act 3, scene 1

◆ Claudius and Gertrude ask Rosencrantz and Guildenstern what they have found out about Hamlet's madness. Ophelia is set up for her "chance" meeting with Hamlet.

◆ Hamlet meditates on suicide and the possibility of an afterlife.

◆ Hamlet and Ophelia meet. Hamlet realizes they are being overheard and suspects she has colluded in this. Ophelia is left distraught by Hamlet's attacks on her.

◆ What Claudius has overheard convinces him that Hamlet has become dangerous. He wants Hamlet removed to England. Polonius persuades the king to allow him to spy once more on Hamlet, at a meeting with his mother.

In a public investigation of Rosencrantz and Guildenstern (witnessed by Gertrude, Polonius, Ophelia, and *lords*) Claudius maintains his air of concern for Hamlet, although we in the audience now believe him to be a dissembling murderer. His conscience is given a jolt when Polonius comments innocently:

> 'Tis too much proved, that with devotion's visage
> And pious action we do sugar o'er
> The devil himself. (lines 53–55)

❍ What is Claudius's reaction to this? What does his *aside* add to our knowledge of his character?

Claudius asks Gertrude to leave so that he and Polonius can eavesdrop on Ophelia and Hamlet. He may wish to save his loving wife from feeling sullied by such deceptions, or he could be afraid that Hamlet might say something which will allude to the murder. He does not know how much of an ally Hamlet may make of Ophelia. Claudius could order Polonius to leave: Ophelia may be the old man's daughter but Claudius is his sovereign. Perhaps Claudius sees Polonius as a possible accomplice in whatever needs to be done to secure his throne, or at least a man who will serve his purposes. Claudius may be clinging to the hope that Hamlet is lovesick and not suspicious of his father's death.

Claudius and Gertrude have acted together so far. Her absence during the eavesdropping episode, and thereby her non-participation in the decision to send Hamlet to England, is the start of a shift in her place in the drama. She is not at Claudius's side as he begins his attack on Hamlet.

Seeing Hamlet approaching, Claudius and Polonius leave Ophelia as bait and withdraw to hiding. There they are treated to the best-known of all Shakespeare's speeches. It is always called a soliloquy, though strictly speaking it isn't, for Ophelia is on stage and within ear-shot. Directors usually contrive the scene so that Hamlet comes on without noticing Ophelia reading her book. ❷ Do you think Claudius and Polonius overhear Hamlet's soliloquy as well as the conversation? What would they make of it?

Imagine being an actor having to deliver a speech which many of the audience can probably recite by heart. It is a great test of acting skill to make it sound fresh and exciting. It must have impact because it is a hugely important moment in the play.

Here is a man who has set in motion a complex plot to trap the king with a play that will be enacted in a few hours' time. He knows that Rosencrantz and Guildenstern are really little more than agents of the king. He is tormented by the damnation that enacting the Ghost's commands will inevitably bring down upon him, and by the possibility that the Ghost may be a devil and not his father's spirit at all. Yet in the midst of all this he delivers a cool, rational, and reflective analysis of death and the afterlife. It shows how analytical the intellectual Hamlet can be. For a supposed madman he is frighteningly cold and in control.

His host of troubles is alluded to in the images *slings and arrows of outrageous fortune* and *a sea of troubles* (lines 66–67). To die, to commit suicide, would be a way of ending these *thousand natural shocks* (line 70). But beyond this most general allusion to the multiplicity of woes that beset him, the whole speech is devoid of personal reference, of self-pity or details of his own situation. There is no mention of other characters, nor of the revenge that torments him. Unlike his other soliloquies, which spring directly from the drama of the play, here Hamlet is coolly musing on a philosophical problem: what might happen to us after we die?

Notice how the poetry reflects this calculating, philosophical mood. The iambic pentameters are beautifully measured, the meaning flows smoothly from one line to the next and the images are clear and well thought out. The whole effect is to show a man in the grip of melancholy but not of passion. His arguments are logical and ordered.

❂ Paraphrase Hamlet's thoughts on the problems of life and the possibility of suicide in a few lines. What does he conclude? Compare his soliloquy with Macbeth's speech in *Macbeth*, Act 1, scene 7, beginning *If it were done*. What similarities are there?

The most passionate outburst comes at the end of the soliloquy when he finally notices Ophelia: *The fair Ophelia!—Nymph, in thy orisons/ Be all my sins remembered* (lines 97–98). That is the only exclamation mark in the whole soliloquy. Notice also the use of the word "fair." Shakespeare uses this word in many other plays and poems to sum up all that is best and most desirable in women. It is a sort of short-hand for honesty, gentleness, and beauty. Hamlet is paying Ophelia a much greater compliment than such a small word suggests.

Hamlet's soft words to Ophelia soon come to an abrupt end. He realizes she is colluding with unseen eavesdroppers. How this scene is played is one of the directorial problems of the play. At what point does Hamlet realize he is being overheard? Most directors opt for a sudden realization around line 141—*Where's your father?* But as Hamlet is growing increasingly aggressive toward her well before this, it may be that he is already aware that Claudius is eavesdropping and only now considers that Polonius may be in on the intrigue as well.

Why is Hamlet driven to such fury toward a girl for whom he is supposed to have had very fond feelings? It could be that he never really had much interest in Ophelia: her passivity throughout the play hardly makes her a character likely to have captivated him. But if we assume that he was once fond of her (he says he loved her in Act 5, scene 1) then his anger may be caused by the betrayal he feels. Her speech is almost obsessively formal throughout their meeting, suggesting that she is aware she is being listened to. This could be an unconscious verbal clue that Hamlet picks up. With this following hard on the confession by Rosencrantz and Guildenstern that they were sent for, Hamlet must feel that so many people he was close to are turning against him. He challenges Ophelia: *Are you honest?* (line 113), and *Are you fair?* (line 115): that key word again.

Deciding that she is most certainly not *fair,* his anger quickly expands into a rant against all women, their faults personified by the hapless and overwhelmed Ophelia. He knows he is being overheard and he may want to provide the hidden listeners with a real madman's rant, but it is nonetheless a vicious attack. It is given an unpleasant edge by Hamlet's focusing on the sexual depravity of women, against which he urges Ophelia to lock herself away in a nunnery. He certainly sounds as if his dislike of women is heartfelt.

The meeting between Hamlet and Ophelia begins (lines 99–120) in fairly formal blank verse. But when Hamlet becomes angry the dialogue shifts to long prose speeches by him, broken by single lines from her. Hamlet's anger is too wild and furious to fit within the rhythmic flow of verse.

○ Compare his *Get thee to a nunnery* and *If thou dost marry* speeches (lines 131–141, 146–152) to his attack on his mother in Act 3, scene 4. What common features do these angry tirades share?

○ Can you find anything in Ophelia's talk with Hamlet to suggest that she has heard Hamlet's soliloquy—a man she is supposed to have loved musing on killing himself?

After Hamlet has stalked off, Ophelia's grief (lines 163–175) seems genuine. It invites us to pity a young girl who up to now we might have regarded as weak and shallow. But if she was hoping for comfort from either Claudius or her father she is disappointed. The king doesn't even acknowledge her and Polonius merely says, tritely, *How now, Ophelia* (line 192). They are preoccupied with Hamlet's mental state. If his outburst against Ophelia was designed to convince the eavesdroppers that he is mad, then it has worked: Claudius readily agrees to Polonius's suggestion that Hamlet be shipped off to England. Notice the potential cruelty in Polonius's suggestion that the king might instead *confine him where/ Your wisdom best shall think* (lines 200–201). Given that we soon learn of the king's murderous intentions towards Hamlet, this can be read as a chilling invitation to wipe his hands of the troublesome prince.

Act 3, scene 2

◆ Hamlet reveals his plan with the play to Horatio.

◆ The court watches the "play within a play." Claudius rushes out.

◆ Hamlet is convinced that the Ghost was speaking the truth and is sworn (again) to revenge.

◆ Hamlet plans to end his friendship with Rosencrantz and Guildenstern.

This is another long scene (432 lines) with several separate episodes.

The scene opens with a long digression (lines 1–53) on theater. Hamlet lectures the First Player on styles of acting. Dramatically, the "reason" for this long aside is simply to guide the actor towards the right way to play "The Murder of Gonzago" before the court. It shows Hamlet to be a keen and knowledgeable theater-goer. But imagine it played on stage before an Elizabethan audience. It would have been a fast and furious commentary on contemporary acting styles, almost certainly played for humorous effect. It would have provided a little light relief before the intense and complex events of the rest of the scene.

When Horatio enters there is a sudden change of mood and style. Hamlet's advice to the First Player is delivered in long prose passages with sentences that run on for several lines; a style that lends itself to speedy comic delivery. With Horatio, Hamlet reverts to blank verse, conveying a much more considered and serious style of delivery. In measured and heartfelt terms Hamlet expresses his admiration for Horatio, who now appears to be his one true friend. He is clearly referring to Horatio when he says *Give me that man/ That is not passion's slave, and I will wear him/ In my heart's core* (lines 76–78): which has a slightly ironic ring given Hamlet's recent impassioned outburst against Ophelia.

Hamlet explains the significance of the murder in the play they are about to see and urges Horatio to watch the king's reaction carefully. He does not tell Horatio the details of what the Ghost has told him, but he does confide much more in Horatio here than he has with anyone else. It is a small step for Horatio to see the play and understand that Hamlet suspects Claudius. Like judges at a competition, they will compare their impressions of Claudius's reaction after the performance. Hamlet returns to the possibility that the Ghost is a devil, and clearly sees Claudius's response to the play as a final test of the validity of his revenge. This raises the dramatic tension in what we are about to see.

The whole court sweeps on stage. After a brief dismissive verbal swipe at Claudius and a labored comic pun at Polonius's expense—*Brutus/brute, Capitol/capital* (lines 109–112)—Hamlet focuses his attentions on Ophelia. His attitude to her has changed completely. Compare the flowing blank verse of his conversation with Horatio to the short "one-liners" of his quick but cutting exchanges with Ophelia. As always, she is completely unable to match his flow of edgy remarks, which focus on sex in crude but thinly veiled terms. He is picking up the theme of sexual depravity in women that colored their previous meeting, but now he appears to be instigating a suppressed bawdiness. He does not attack her, but teases, feigns affection and confuses her. In the eyes of Claudius this must seem as if the "madness" he and Polonius overheard so recently is continuing with precisely the same cause—sex/unrequited love—as before.

In other Shakespeare plays such lewd banter is given to clowns, peasants, and servants, but here a prince is speaking of *country matters*. It adds yet more layers to Hamlet's complex character. He may be still feigning madness from unrequited love and now sexual frustration, or it may be that, as a young man and a prince he feels able to indulge in sexual banter with a young woman. Either way, it contrasts with the cool intellectual and the tortured, undecided revenger we have seen in other scenes.

The dumbshow by the Players puts an end to Hamlet's exchanges with Ophelia before passions can run amok. A dumbshow explaining what the audience were about to see in a play was a common device in Elizabethan theater. But it raises the first of two problems with the "play within a play." If Claudius sees the murder enacted in dumbshow, why does he not react then? It has been suggested by some critics that Shakespeare intended to suggest that Claudius could see his crime replicated before him once, but not a second time in the actual play.

Another ingenious explanation of the dumbshow has to do with the staging, and watching, of this complex scene. We have an audience on stage watching a play. The real audience out in the theater needs to watch the "play within a play," but more importantly (for Hamlet and Horatio have just discussed this) has to watch the court audience for the king's reaction. Shakespeare could have been aware of this splitting of the audience's attention. He provided the dumbshow so that they could focus on the king and the court when "The Murder of Gonzago" was played, and not worry too much about following the drama as they already broadly knew its content. Whatever the reason, this phase of the scene is complex and difficult to direct. To understand the full dramatic effect you have to imagine it staged.

"The Murder of Gonzago," the "play within a play," gives Shakespeare a chance to add another style of writing to this scene. If most of the asides in *Hamlet* about theater are critical, here there is no more than a gentle dig at a style of formal verse theater that was already largely obsolete when *Hamlet* was first performed. An Elizabethan audience would have recognized an earlier dramatic style in the endless rhyming couplets of the play (lines 177–252). It is interesting to compare this obsessive, unvarying pattern to the fluid and inventive use of the same iambic measure in speeches such as Hamlet's *O, what a rogue and peasant slave am I* (Act 2, scene 2, lines 577–634). In "The Murder of Gonzago" Shakespeare makes an excellent pastiche of this earlier, more rigid style of dramatic verse.

The arrival of the poisoner (Third Player or Lucianus) raises the dramatic quality of the "play within a play." His speech beginning *Thoughts black, hands apt, drugs fit and time agreeing* (lines 280–281) blows away the air of comic pastiche and prepares us for the drama that will explode when Claudius reacts to the murder. It also contrasts with the exchanges between Hamlet and Ophelia (sexual innuendo again) and between Hamlet and Gertrude, where the latter comments on the queen in the play: *The lady doth protest too much, methinks* (line 254). Is this a throw-away comment made to placate her mad son who has set himself up unopposed as a commentator between the Players and the court? Or does Gertrude's remark suggest that she sees how the queen in the play is cast in a role mimicking her own, and that she is becoming disconcerted by the way the story is developing?

She storms out with her husband and the rest of the court when, unable to bear seeing an exact depiction of his crime, the guilt-ridden Claudius curtails the performance. At this point we must consider the second crucial problem with "The Murder of Gonzago": have we already heard the extra speech that Hamlet wrote and had inserted into the text? It is probable that we haven't, but if Shakespeare had already plotted for Claudius to storm off having heard only part of the play, why bother with all the fuss about instructing the First Player to learn extra lines?

There could be another way of looking at Claudius's abrupt exit. It is unlikely that anyone else in the court (except possibly Gertrude) would ever think that Claudius had committed regicide and fratricide to gain the throne. He is a skilled and diplomatic king: probably a relief to some courtiers after the axe-wielding battle hero Old Hamlet! He is not being exposed in the eyes of the court. But Hamlet has been insulting Claudius all evening. Suddenly deciding that the play is called "The Mousetrap," Hamlet is alluding to how he imagines, or knows, that Claudius refers to Gertrude as his *mouse* (see Act 3, scene 4, line 205). Hamlet's remarks about murder and revenge (lines 287–290) seem extreme comments on what is supposed to be a mere theatrical diversion. It could be that Hamlet's attitude is an attempt to rouse the king so that he strikes first and thus sweeps away all Hamlet's indecisions in the matter of revenge. The king chooses to exit rather than confront Hamlet and expose himself.

Whatever the cause, the king is *marvellous distempered* (lines 327–328). Hamlet is now sure that Claudius is guilty of his father's murder. The revenger is finally convinced. He will *take the ghost's word for a thousand pound* (lines 312–313). He seems elated in his certainty; in his excitement forgetting his earlier fears that revengers inevitably condemn themselves by completing the act of revenge. His wild glee contrasts with Horatio's more sober agreement that what they have seen suggests the king's guilt.

When Rosencrantz and Guildenstern re-enter with Gertrude's message there is more bitter sparring between them and Hamlet. The passage in which he tries to make Guildenstern play the recorder culminates in Hamlet effectively ending the friendship he had with his two school friends. While there is a thin veneer of comedy here, there is a steely edge to Hamlet's words.

Hamlet's baiting of Polonius is less edgy: his attitude to the statesman is simply one of disdain. But at the end of the scene Hamlet's more violent mental state comes bursting out: *Now I could drink hot blood* (lines 422–423). But notice that he does not *do such bitter business as the day/ Would quake to look on* (lines 424–325). Instead, like a dutiful son, he answers his mother's summons, even avoiding killing Claudius along the way. The course toward revenge may have been set by the king's reaction to the play, but Hamlet is still no simple blood-driven revenge hero.

○ What parallels can you draw between the theatrical court entertainment in this scene and the "entertainment" of the fencing match between Hamlet and Laertes in the final scene?

Act 3, scene 3

◆ Claudius orders Rosencrantz and Guildenstern to be Hamlet's guards on his enforced journey to England.
◆ Claudius confesses his crime in prayer.
◆ On his way to visit his mother, Hamlet comes across Claudius praying, but does not kill him.

The dramatic drive of this scene is in the rushed planning and confusion that now reigns in the castle. There is a sense in the opening phase (lines 1–27) that Claudius is frantically, mechanically, trying to deal with the practicalities of securing his own position. He is still expertly delegating and it is likely that no one in the court knows why he is so shocked and upset. If they look for a reason it will be in Hamlet's "mad" behavior, not the play. Claudius can still be regarded as a capable leader trying to secure the court from the dangers of a mad stepson.

Rosencrantz and Guildenstern have quickly moved from being rejected by Hamlet to accepting a commission to be, effectively, his jailers, although they don't necessarily know they are taking him toward his intended death. Polonius is still fulfilling the role of schemer and spy. It is his idea to listen in on Gertrude's conversation with Hamlet.

Claudius's confession, alone at prayer, suddenly reveals the depth of his despair. His soliloquy (if we assume that God is not listening!) powerfully invites our sympathy at precisely the moment where, in a typical revenge tragedy, the villain would be prepared for receiving his "just desserts." It is also the first and only moment in the play when we hear Claudius's guilt from his own lips. Claudius may be a murderer, but he is also a suffering human being. This is a masterful piece of character development and raises the stakes in the revenger–victim conflict. But while we feel for his pain, we must remember that Claudius never considers giving up the things he has gained by the murder, although it is precisely because he still has the throne and is married to Gertrude, because he still enjoys the fruits of the murder, that he knows he is damned.

Yet he still excites our pity. He is a flawed man who has created an impossible dilemma for himself. What if he did love Gertrude so much, and she him, that he murdered for love of her? Would he seem less of a villain? ❷ How does our limited knowledge of Old Hamlet, Claudius's victim, affect our attitude to Claudius at this point? Could the quality of his reign make him less of a villain?

Hamlet could easily kill Claudius now. He is carrying a sword: Claudius is distracted and unarmed. ❷ List the lives that might be saved if Hamlet exacted his revenge now.

Think about this and the following scene on stage. Think about props and costume. Claudius and most of the court are often dressed to present themselves as "modernists": they do not carry weapons. But Hamlet is now wandering about the castle with a sword or dagger. This is a device that is important in the next scene, when Gertrude fears attack. Carrying a visible weapon underlines Hamlet as a danger to those who have wronged him. Add to this his extremely agitated state since the play broke up in disarray and we have an urgent sense of impending violence as this scene draws to a close. Maybe Hamlet, despite being proved right about the murder of his father, is a little crazy. If we were Claudius, even a Claudius innocent of Old Hamlet's murder, would we not want Hamlet safely out of the way?

But Claudius is guilty: he has confessed, and by confessing, he is in a state of grace. Even though Hamlet doesn't hear the content of Claudius's prayers, he will not kill him now because a man killed while penitently praying will go to heaven. Hamlet remembers the Ghost's graphic descriptions of the purgatorial torments he faces each day because he was killed without a chance to confess: *With all my imperfections on my head* (Act 1, scene 5, line 86). Hamlet does not want Claudius to escape any of the torments of purgatory, so he will not, despite a perfect opportunity to gain revenge, *do it pat* (line 78).

There are two other alternative explanations for Hamlet's inaction at this point. He may still, despite his claims to being absolutely certain that Claudius is guilty, be prey to his old indecision and inability to act decisively. And he may also be aware that, as murders go, killing an unarmed man at prayer is about as low as a murderer can get. He will certainly damn himself if he kills Claudius now.

Act 3, scene 4

◆ Hamlet tries to persuade Gertrude that her marriage to Claudius is wrong.
◆ Hamlet kills Polonius, who is hiding in Gertrude's room to eavesdrop.
◆ Gertrude appears to recognize the wrongness of what she has done; or could be convinced that Hamlet is actually mad and be simply humoring him.

This scene is set in Gertrude's *closet*. Many productions take this to be her bedroom and a bed often features prominently, highlighting the Oedipal tendencies that are undoubtedly there in Hamlet's character. He has already more than once dwelt upon imagining Claudius and Gertrude in bed. But there is a danger in seeing this scene as being obviously set to reveal a perverse Oedipal drive bursting forth from Hamlet. A *closet* is not a bedroom but a private room. Gertrude need not be dressed for bed, but can be dressed as she was at the play, and be sitting in a room designed for the quite formal business of receiving private guests. As written by Shakespeare it is not a bedroom scene at all, but a private meeting between mother and son.

None the less there is something strange and perverse in Hamlet's attitude towards his mother. In Act 5, scene 1, we are told that Hamlet is 30. A man of this age instructing his mother in the details of how she can avoid intimacy in bed with her husband hints at the unnatural to say the least!

Hamlet's revulsion at the sexual intimacy Gertrude has apparently enjoyed and indeed delighted in up to now, and his dwelling on details of it, taint what could otherwise be a potentially reasonable appeal to his mother: how can you prefer Claudius to Old Hamlet? As with everything in this play, Shakespeare provides many levels of meaning.

One could devote pages of commentary to the many threads that run through this lengthy and crucial meeting between Gertrude and her son. It is the only time in the play they are alone together (after Polonius's death). It is the one time he can pour out his heart to his mother, who, we rapidly discover, is clearly the most important woman in the world to him.

Gertrude and Hamlet begin (lines 11–29) by bickering. Their exchanges are short and nastily witty:

QUEEN: *Come, come, you answer with an idle tongue.*
HAMLET: *Go, go, you question with a wicked tongue.*
   (lines 14–15)

Continuing with this level of dialogue would not allow things to develop very far. But when Hamlet kills Polonius, assuming the unseen eavesdropper to be Claudius, the style of language changes completely. Hamlet lays out his case to Gertrude logically, in neat blank verse. He employs a wide range of passionate but controlled imagery. He has two themes in the conversation with his mother up to the point where the Ghost appears: the unnaturalness of Gertrude's marriage and the unfavorable comparison of Claudius to his father.

The reason for Polonius's discovery and death is his cry in response to Gertrude's fear that she will be murdered (her cry for help, line 26–27). There is nothing in the text to indicate what suddenly makes her fear for her life. Directors usually refer back to the fact that Hamlet is wandering about with an unconcealed weapon. Some action with this might cause Gertrude's sudden alarm.

Hamlet seems strangely untroubled by the murder. For a man who has debated so long with himself over the justification of killing his father's murderer, the slaying of an innocent man seems to have little effect on him. He mentions that the murder is not as bad as killing a king and marrying his brother. He is telling Gertrude for the first time that her first husband was murdered, but it does not seem to make much impact. The thread is quickly dropped. When Gertrude next sees Claudius her feelings for him seem unchanged. Hamlet's revelation of the murder, strangely combined with the marriage into one act, is almost a throw-away. One wonders if Gertrude really understands what he has said.

Hamlet sees both the marriage and Claudius himself as corrupt and corrupting. The marriage *sets a blister* (line 53) on the *fair forehead of innocent love* (line 52). Claudius is described as a *mildewed ear* (line 74). The long "comparison" speech (lines 63–98) is usually played with Hamlet having two pictures to hand, one of Claudius and one of his father. The emotional pitch rises throughout the speech. Hamlet begins by appearing quite rational, if totally biased. He ends in a rage, having once again strayed back to images of sex between his mother and Claudius.

From line 103 to the arrival of the Ghost, Hamlet rants against Gertrude's sexual activities in gross and perverse terms for a grown son to use to his mother. Her repeated wish to hear no more may reflect not that he has convinced her of her sins, but that she is appalled at the tone of her son's attack. Hamlet's rage prompts the arrival of the Ghost, who warns Hamlet to remember his instruction not to harm his widow. The Ghost reminds Hamlet of his oath to exact revenge, which he sees as an *almost blunted purpose* (line 127).

○ What images does Hamlet use to praise his dead father in lines 63–73? Make sure you understand them.

Hamlet becomes softer, almost apologetic, toward his mother when the Ghost departs. But her reactions to Hamlet have been distorted by witnessing him speaking in terror to the empty air, for she cannot see the Ghost. This is an interesting plot device. The Ghost has been visible to many people already: to Horatio and others on the watch. Yet it is invisible to its widow.

○ Is the Ghost deliberately hiding itself so as not to cause distress to one it loved in life? Is it really the devil assuming Old Hamlet's form, choosing, at the one moment when its appearance might have won Hamlet's case for him with his mother, to be fussy over who can see it? Or is the Ghost purely in Hamlet's imagination now?

The Ghost's appearance to Hamlet alone has grave consequences. There is a sense in the concluding section of the scene, from the Ghost's exit to the end, that Gertrude could be humoring a son who has just proved himself mad and homicidal. The key line is Gertrude's *O Hamlet, thou has cleft my heart in twain* (line 177). There is a crucial decision to be made in the way this line is interpreted, for both readers and directors of productions.

Hamlet may have convinced Gertrude of the utter wrongness of what she has done. She could be stunned into near silence by sudden and overwhelming guilt. She therefore humbly allows Hamlet great space (line 178 onward) to lecture her soberly and logically on a course of abstinence from intimacy with her new husband. Gertrude merely gives single lines of assent. He has won her over.

But Gertrude appears blissfully in love with Claudius. We never hear cross words between them. Would she be convinced of the marriage's utter wrongness on the word of someone who has just killed Polonius, spoken with empty air, and dwelt with perverse intensity on her private sexual habits? Is it a mother's heart that is broken by seeing her only son going completely mad? She listens with patience, sorrow, and perhaps even fear to Hamlet's lengthy account of how she must forswear Claudius's affections, and to his lame justification for killing Polonius in error. There is much skillful thinking and explanation on Hamlet's part, but it might not convince Gertrude at all.

To her, and to many of us in the audience, Hamlet at this point is mad, obsessed with his mother's sexuality and driven to murdering unseen victims. If Hamlet does ever descend into genuine madness at any time in the play, this is the moment—and the madness continues for the following two scenes.

Whichever interpretation you favor, there is a strange dislocation between the Hamlet we see here, who will soon career about the castle evading pursuit, and the strangely sober and philosophical man who returns from his abridged sea voyage. There is a climax of tension and fury in Hamlet's character at this point that is never repeated in the play.

One final point to note about Gertrude is that when she next sees Claudius, having promised Hamlet to abstain from any intimacy with him, almost her first words are to say that her son is *Mad as the sea and wind when both contend/ Which is the mightier* (Act 4, scene 1, lines 7–8). She does not protest at his being sent into exile.

Test yourself

? It is hard to gauge what Gertrude is thinking throughout Acts 4 and 5 because she is never given a soliloquy in which she can reveal her thoughts and feelings. What do you think Gertrude feels about Hamlet at the end of Act 3? Draw a Mini Mind Map showing the things you would want her to say and explain in a soliloquy.

? Make a Mini Mind Map of all Hamlet's references to sexual depravity in this Act.

Test your knowledge

1 Who consider themselves *lawful espials*?
2 What is the country from which *no traveller returns*?
3 What is Ophelia trying to return to Hamlet?
4 What kind of man does Hamlet tell Ophelia she should marry, if she must marry?
5 Who is *metal more attractive*?
6 What does Hamlet call the play?
7 What might Hamlet *do pat*?
8 Polonius's murder is a *bloody deed*, almost as bad as what?
9 Who claims they *must be cruel only to be kind*?
10 Who was *a foolish prating knave*?
(Answers, see p. 92)

This is where the intermission usually comes—so take a break now before Act 4.

Act 4, scene 1

◆ Gertrude and Claudius discuss what Hamlet has done.

Notice how Rosencrantz and Guildenstern enter with Claudius and Gertrude, and how, despite Claudius's politeness to them—*Friends both* (line 34), *I pray you haste* (line 38)—they are dispatched like servants to do his work.

Up to now the king and queen have appeared loving and have acted in unison. Now they are less than honest with one another. Claudius asks Gertrude to explain—*translate* (line 2)—her distress. She tells him what has happened, but says nothing of Hamlet's claim that her first husband was murdered. Either she is beginning to suspect the truth and does not want Claudius to know, or she may have disregarded what Hamlet said as the ravings of a madman. In this scene, and in the remainder of the play, her interactions with Claudius contain nothing to suggest that she has been affected by anything Hamlet has said. But there is a sense of growing distance between herself and her husband.

Claudius paints a picture of Hamlet as a dangerous, criminal lunatic: a threat to anyone and everyone at court. He cannot share with Gertrude the truth about the murder he committed, nor that he is now certain that Hamlet knows about it. But in killing Polonius, Hamlet has given Claudius the perfect excuse he needs to send Hamlet away.

Act 4, scenes 2–3

◆ Hamlet leads Rosencrantz and Guildenstern on a chase around the castle.
◆ Hamlet is sent away to England.
◆ Claudius reveals he has sent Hamlet to his death.

These two scenes follow on immediately from one another and can be read as one continuous episode in the plot.

The comedy in these scenes provides a dramatic contrast to the intensity of the recent closet scene (Act 3, scene 4). Try to imagine it on stage, with Hamlet dashing off and being pursued. Notice how Claudius speaks in blank verse while Hamlet's lines are all prose. It underlines Claudius's authority. Hamlet is literally on the run, and when he is captured makes no attempt to question his being sent to England. Claudius is the voice of command in these two brief scenes. Hamlet's verbal tricks achieve nothing.

Despite playing a role in the overheard conversation with Ophelia, organizing the play, and murdering Polonius, Hamlet is actually no nearer to achieving revenge. Perhaps he thinks the journey may offer new possibilities for gaining it. In the closet scene he hinted at plans he has made to counter a conspiracy against him involving Rosencrantz and Guildenstern (Act 3, scene 4, lines 225–240). But his return to Denmark appears to happen by pure chance, so it's not clear what ideas he has at this point for turning the journey to his advantage in the pursuit of revenge against Claudius.

In his seemingly mad, comic speeches, Hamlet lets us know that he understands how far Rosencrantz and Guildenstern are puppets of the king. He calls Rosencrantz a sponge *that soaks up the King's countenance, his rewards, his authorities* (lines 15–16). Then he leads them off on a chase about the castle.

Scene 3 opens with him being brought before Claudius. We do not see him captured by Rosencrantz and Guildenstern, and it is interesting to consider how much of a fight he might have put up: this is an armed man who has just murdered Polonius. He may have allowed himself to be caught to put his counter-plan into action. Hamlet maintains his tone of comic madness throughout his interview with Claudius, but there is so much cunning in what he says that it is hard to believe he is genuinely crazed at this point. Rather he is using his quick wits to mock the king.

Left alone on stage at the end of scene 3, Claudius reveals that he is sending Hamlet to his death. This is the conspiracy Hamlet suspects. Claudius's brief soliloquy reveals his anger. Compared to his tone at prayer in Act 3, scene 3, he is full of violence. He may be racked with guilt, but he will fight, and plot murder, to secure his position. He is a villain after all.

Act 4, scene 4

◆ Hamlet sees an army led by Fortinbras marching to fight a pointless war. He meditates on the nature of honor.

This is the first scene since Act 2 set outside the castle. Some productions of the play cut all but the first eight lines. One justification for this is that the scene adds nothing to the plot, and though Hamlet has a long and beautifully poetic soliloquy (lines 34–69), it conveys nothing new about his state of mind or intentions. He compares himself to the soldiers just as he did to the Players, and again finds himself less driven than they are in their actions.

But the scene serves to show Hamlet yet again how other men are prepared to act and take risks with very little purpose or justification; while he, with a murdered father to avenge, does nothing. It can be seen as a more warlike version of the First Player moving himself to tears in Act 2, scene 2.

The soliloquy shows us that Hamlet is not (now anyway) mad. He meditates in beautifully measured blank verse. He is

moved by the sacrifice the army is about to make, but his

emotions are controlled. His analytical, intellectual voice has returned. His tone lets us know that he is someone Rosencrantz and Guildenstern ought not to underestimate. Its conclusion hints at the fate that awaits them:

> *O, from this time forth*
> *My thoughts be bloody, or be nothing worth!* (lines 68–69)

Fortinbras invades Poland!

? Imagine you are a newspaper journalist reporting Fortinbras's campaign against Poland. Write a short tabloid news item using the basic information given by the Captain and enlarged upon by Hamlet, describing what is happening. Your piece must convey the same opinion of the war they go to fight as Hamlet holds.

Act 4, scene 5

◆ Gertrude speaks of her foreboding and unhappiness.
◆ Ophelia, driven mad by grief, talks and sings in a confused way about love.
◆ Laertes bursts into the court, threatening Claudius and demanding to know why his father died.
◆ Claudius defuses Laertes's anger but they are interrupted by a second appearance of the mad Ophelia.

The responses of Polonius's children to his death control much of the drama from now on.

We do not know exactly why Gertrude is unwilling to speak with Ophelia. Assuming Gertrude knows she has been driven mad, she may wish to avoid Ophelia, either because she does not want another confrontation with madness, or she may be sick with guilt, knowing that her son is the cause of the girl's condition. There is a three-line appearance by Horatio (lines 18–20). He offers decent advice to the queen: see Ophelia to dispel any rumors (of the cause of the madness?) in *ill breeding minds*. Why Horatio needs to speak these lines is not clear: probably it is a simple dramatic device to remind us that he is still about the court even though Hamlet has gone.

Gertrude's brief aside (lines 22–25) is the nearest she comes to a soliloquy but she tells us no more than we can reasonably assume: that events at court have left her with a feeling of impending doom in her *sick soul.*

Ophelia's madness, in both her appearances in this scene, reflects her character. She does not rage: she is distracted and submissive. Hers is the craziness of a simple child. Unlike Hamlet's "madness" there is no real *method* in her snatches of songs. But there are clear themes running through her mind: loss of a loved one and unhappiness in love or unrequited affection. That being frustrated in love has caused this madness is suggested by her mixture of pretty rhymes and bawdiness.
○ How does Ophelia's madness alter the view we may have had of her up to now?

Tension rises when a messenger arrives warning Claudius to save himself from a furious Laertes who is returned from Paris and has broken into the court supported by a *rabble.* For the first time we hear about the ordinary citizens of Denmark. Claudius has seemed such an assured ruler that it comes as a shock to learn that ordinary citizens are ready and eager to flock to support Laertes as a challenger to the throne. Perhaps beyond the court as well as within it *something is rotten in the state of Denmark.* Notice how Gertrude instantly rises to her husband's defense (lines 119–120 and again at line 146).

Claudius shows the control and authority he demonstrated in Act 1 when he calmly outfaces Laertes. The pitch of their confrontation is declining, thanks to Claudius's smooth words, when they are interrupted by Ophelia's second appearance. Again her madness is distracted and almost picturesque. The flower symbolism emphasizes this. She alludes to her dead father, suggesting that his death has pushed her into madness.

When she wanders off again Claudius dives in to defuse any chance of a second outburst of anger from Laertes. The younger man is no match for the king's convincing reasonableness. Laertes is too gullible. When Claudius offers to hand over the throne if he is found to be implicated in Polonius's murder, anyone less innocent than Laertes would suspect something: Claudius's gesture is too extravagant. But in a sense Claudius speaks the truth: he did have no part in the murder. ✪ Do you think Claudius already knows he has an ally in Laertes? How?

Act 4, scene 6

◆ Via a letter to Horatio, we learn that Hamlet has escaped from Rosencrantz and Guildenstern and is back in Denmark.

The letter to Horatio fulfills two functions. It allows a lot of action to be simply reported (action that would be difficult to stage), and it shows the transformed state of Hamlet's mind. He never plays the madman to Horatio. The tone of the letter prepares us for the return of a calmer, more philosophical Hamlet in Act 5.

The story of Hamlet's escape from exile (and death) in England sounds rather far-fetched. Why should the pirates treat him well? Because he is to do them a favor—but we never learn what that favor is. As when the Players readily agree to learn new lines for him, Hamlet seems too easily supported by everyone with whom he comes into contact outside the court. But we do learn from Claudius (Act 4, scene 7, lines 20–23) that Hamlet is much loved by the ordinary people of Denmark, so there is some attempt to make the pirates' generosity just a little less implausible. ✪ How believable do you find the help which Hamlet receives?

The structural purpose of the scene is to give a sense of some brief time passing: time in which we can imagine Claudius and Laertes off-stage cementing their alliance against Hamlet. Hamlet requests Horatio to join him with all speed. Horatio is now back from the sidelines and joining Hamlet in the forefront of the action.

Act 4, scene 7

◆ Claudius and Laertes become allies, plotting Hamlet's death.
◆ Gertrude describes Ophelia's drowning.

Claudius does seem to have used the time well. Laertes is not only an ally but a willing and almost subservient one in the plot that Claudius has hatched. On one point only is Laertes unconvinced: why no action (more extreme than exile presumably) was taken against Hamlet immediately after Polonius's murder. The reply is telling: because of *the great love the general gender bear him* (line 20). Now it could be that Claudius is simply inventing an excuse for doing nothing, but it seems more likely that the public really does admire Hamlet (Laertes should be able to verify this), even to the point of supporting him against the king. This reveals an aspect of Hamlet we see nowhere else: the high regard he enjoys as a public figure. ✪ Look at lines 23–26. What is Claudius afraid of here?

Notice the neat and fluid poetry of Claudius's opening speech of this scene (lines 1–26). The language gives the impression that he has regained his sense of command. He is using the weapon he excels with: his brain.

A cryptic note from Hamlet spurs Claudius and Laertes to plot the details of how they plan to kill Hamlet in a rigged fencing match. Claudius has already mentioned how *The Queen his mother/ Lives almost by his looks* (lines 13–14). In plotting to kill Hamlet in her presence, Claudius is beginning to open the rift between himself and Gertrude that will result in both their deaths. ✪ How might Hamlet's absence have affected the queen and her view of the court? Might she begin to suspect that Hamlet was telling the truth about his father's murder?

There is very much a sense that Claudius is testing Laertes's resolve (and possibly his gullibility) as they plot Hamlet's demise. The nature of their relationship from now on is underlined when Claudius asks Laertes directly *Will you be ruled by me?* (line 66). Laertes agrees. His thirst for revenge is guided by Claudius until, after further probing, Laertes confirms that he is so fixed on their plot against Hamlet that he would be prepared *To cut his throat i'th'church!* (line 144). This is ironic, given that Hamlet would not kill Claudius at prayer. Claudius never even hints at why he wants Hamlet dead.

✪ Family loyalty and honor are matters of life and death for Laertes. What does it say about him that he so readily believes Claudius is willing to plot his stepson's death to avenge the deaths of Polonius and Ophelia? Why doesn't Laertes think about the family loyalties that Claudius might have?

As with his first speech in this scene, Claudius has spoken throughout in quite long passages of carefully worded and evenly measured blank verse. His reasonable voice has entirely persuaded Laertes into doing his evil business against Hamlet. ❍ What are the main differences between Claudius and Laertes as they appear so far (up to line 186) in this scene?

Their lengthy conversation is interrupted by the arrival of Gertrude, who reports in great detail the death by drowning of poor, mad Ophelia. She died as she lived, unable to rouse herself to action. Gertrude could give a much simpler report of Ophelia's death. The plot does not require that we know every detail. This very long play is already three-quarters over and events are clearly heading toward a climax.

Gertrude's speech (lines 190–208) sounds out of character. It is highly formal, stylized, and poetic. It is not the sort of discourse you would have with the brother of a girl who has just drowned herself. But it is a marvellous piece of lyric poetry! More than any other Shakespeare play, *Hamlet* contains an enormous variety of writing styles. It is a showcase for the range of the author's genius. Gertrude's lament for Ophelia, though dramatically unnecessary, is inspired. It is full of glorious visual imagery. The tone, while melancholic, is enlivened with extravagant, fairytale description. It is too sweet and flowery—the girl is mad and drowning, for heaven's sake! —but it is a description of a scene of almost pastoral beauty before the grim graveside humor and general slaughter of Act 5 gets underway. In its dreamy, ethereal tone it is a perfect epitaph for the harmless, light-as-a-wisp and tragic Ophelia. ❍ Who or what does Gertrude blame for Ophelia's death? Why is she hedging away from describing it as suicide?

Note Claudius's lines that close the scene; it is the voice of a businessman who has set up a shady deal and now risks seeing it fall apart!

Test yourself

? Draw a Mini Mind Map showing Claudius's thoughts and preoccupations throughout this scene.

Test your knowledge

Beside each of these quotes from Act 4 put (a) the name of the speaker, (b) who they are speaking about.

1 *Mad as the sea and wind when both contend/ Which is the mightier.*

2 *If your messenger find him not there, seek him i'th'other place yourself.*

3 *That for a fantasy and trick of fame/ Go to their graves like beds.*

4 *'Twere good she were spoken with, for she may strew/ Dangerous conjectures in ill-breeding minds.*

5 *How cheerfully on the false trail they cry!/ O, this is counter, you false Danish dogs!*

6 *How came he dead? I'll not be juggled with.*

7 *But let him come./ It warms the very sickness in my heart/ That I shall live and tell him to his teeth ...*

8 *How much I had to do to calm his rage!*

(Answers, see p. 92)

Take a break before digging into the graveyard scene!

Act 5, scene 1

◆ Overheard by Hamlet and Horatio, the two Gravediggers discuss a possible suicide who is being buried in consecrated ground.

◆ Hamlet confronts the First Gravedigger. They debate how death makes everyone equal.

◆ Hamlet examines Yorick's skull, and meditates on death as the "great leveller" of mankind.

◆ Ophelia's funeral procession approaches. Hamlet and Horatio watch from a hiding place.

◆ Laertes quarrels with the priest, who will perform only minimal holy offices because Ophelia's death is *doubtful.*

◆ Gertrude expresses her now-dashed hope that Ophelia and Hamlet might have married.

◆ Laertes says farewell to his sister in a theatrical show of grief. This angers Hamlet, who emerges to mock Laertes. Hamlet declares that he loved Ophelia. They fight.

♦ Claudius seizes the incident to urge Laertes on in the plot to kill Hamlet.

Note that in some editions the Gravediggers are referred to as *Clowns*. But they are usually described as *Gravediggers*.

A long scene of over 300 lines. The first 180 are primarily comic: full of riddles, songs, and banter, first between the Gravediggers, then between Hamlet and the First Gravedigger. He and Hamlet are sparring partners in a macabre debate full of literally grave humor. Their opinions form a common bond around line 180, when Hamlet is shown the skull of Yorick, the king's jester. Only the final 90 or so lines of the scene are completely devoid of grim humor and have anything to do with developing the plot, principally by heightening the antipathy between Laertes and Hamlet. ❂ Why might Shakespeare have wanted such a big comic interlude at this point in the play's dramatic development?

Notice the usual separation of prose and blank verse. The two Gravediggers, and Hamlet when he is speaking with them, converse entirely in prose, but when the funeral arrives the dialogue is all in blank verse.

Lines 1–62 set up the Gravediggers like music hall comedians, with the First Gravedigger as the lead humorist and his companion being the dim-witted "stooge." The First Gravedigger takes the lead; the Second Gravedigger is the dunce who cannot fathom his riddles or comic arguments.

Shakespeare has created in the First Gravedigger a character who has become a stock figure in many types of literature. He is first in a long line of fictional characters who are jolly and irreverent while engaged in grim occupations. When Hamlet debates with the First Gravedigger we see the prince talking easily and lightly with a commoner, echoing his affable speech with the Players in Act 2, scene 2. It shows us that the prince relates without formality to "ordinary people."

The First Gravedigger wins Hamlet's grudging admiration. He stands outside the court and its intrigues. He sees people age and die, and he buries them. Their rank, sex, and reputation are of no interest to him: he knows they will all rot and turn to dust. He is timeless; engaged in a job that both he and Hamlet know will always be required. He never asks who Hamlet is, and he feels no need to show any special respect towards him. The Gravedigger is happy in his grim work. He is in charge of the scene, and Hamlet can take part if he chooses. Although Hamlet may have the wits to run circles around him, the Gravedigger gets the better of their comic exchanges. Hamlet seems to be enjoying himself. The Gravedigger puts up more opposition in their skirmish of words than Polonius or Rosencrantz and Guildenstern ever did.

But Hamlet's mood becomes darker—not melancholic but philosophical—when the Gravedigger hands him the skull of Yorick. It prompts his famous speech on mortality (lines 190–202), reinforcing with more emotion the meditation on the inevitability of death he has already spoken over another (unknown) skull (lines 100–114). The transience of life is a theme that has been running under the grim humor of the scene up to the discovery of Yorick's skull: now it entirely occupies Hamlet's thoughts. Humor is forgotten. It leads him to consider that even the greatest leaders of men will end up as these poor remains that the Gravedigger flings about. Hamlet realizes that no amount of wealth and power can make a man immortal. The tone is set for the arrival of Ophelia's funeral procession.

Although he has so far done nothing to demonstrate it, Hamlet sounds like a changed man. Exactly what has caused this shift in his personality in so short an absence is unclear, but we sense even in this grimly comic scene that the desire for revenge is not burning so hot now. Conversely, his new calmness suggests he may act more decisively to achieve it.

For centuries, the Christian Church refused to bury suicides in consecrated ground, nor would the deceased be given a full funeral service. Ophelia is being buried at night and with the minimum of ceremony. As the gloomy procession approaches, the open grave becomes the center of a much grimmer drama than the macabre comedy that has accompanied its digging. Ophelia's body is laid in it, Gertrude drops flowers over her, Laertes, in a theatrical and excessive show of grief, jumps into it, and he and Hamlet wrestle in it. The sombre, sad little funeral descends from pathos to brawling. Even now Ophelia herself is sidelined.

Laertes's combative attitude to the churlish Priest sets him up as a man ready to challenge those who pay no respect to his situation as wronged son and brother. He is a "loose cannon," a danger to those who cross him. Perhaps Hamlet ought to have more respect for Laertes's feelings at his sister's funeral. In terms of the plot, he does not need to goad Laertes to provoke a confrontation now. Maybe Hamlet has been shocked by Gertrude's sad remark *I hoped thou shouldst have been my Hamlet's wife* (line 255); maybe Hamlet suddenly realizes he really did love Ophelia. Certainly his outburst, *I loved Ophelia. Forty thousand brothers/ Could not with all their quantity of love/ Make up my sum* (lines 285–287), more than suggests a sudden and belated realization of his feelings.

What ceremony else?

Dramatically, however, the argument and brawl between Hamlet and Laertes in the grave does raise the stakes for their final confrontation. Hamlet's outburst against Laertes provides Claudius with a further chance to remind Laertes of the way they have plotted to gain revenge upon Hamlet.

❍ Draw a Mini Mind Map showing every character present at Ophelia's funeral, and say in one or two words what their feelings and motives are.

Act 5, scene 2

◆ Hamlet explains to Horatio how he opened Claudius's instructions and discovered he was being sent to his death, and how he substituted another set, sealed with his father's ring, condemning Rosencrantz and Guildenstern to death.
◆ Osrick brings Hamlet the challenge of a fencing match with Laertes. Hamlet mocks the courtier but accepts the challenge.
◆ Alone with Horatio, Hamlet expresses a sense of foreboding and unease about the contest. But he also expresses a resigned acceptance of death.
◆ The fencing match. Gertrude drinks the poisoned cup, watched by a horrified Claudius who doesn't prevent her for fear of his plot being discovered. She dies.
◆ Laertes and Hamlet are both wounded by the poisoned sword. Dying, Laertes reveals the plot and blames Claudius —whom Hamlet kills. Hamlet dies in Horatio's arms.
◆ Fortinbras and the English ambassadors arrive simultaneously. Rosencrantz and Guildenstern have been executed. Horatio vows to give Fortinbras a full account of events. Fortinbras orders a soldier's funeral for Hamlet.

A long scene of nearly 450 lines that is almost two separate scenes with very different atmospheres. Up to roughly line 208 we have a physically static scene between Hamlet and Horatio, with the comic character Osrick providing a humorous interlude. After the arrival of the court the scene is one of action, with violent swordplay and four deaths.

This first half of the scene itself divides into three episodes. First we have Hamlet explaining to Horatio how he managed to return to Denmark despite the plans of the king, and how he sent Rosencrantz and Guildenstern to their doom by altering the death warrant they were carrying for him. Hamlet appears to have absolutely no doubt or regret about sending his former friends to their deaths: they were seemingly happy to convey Hamlet to his. But there is a nice twist here. Claudius never (in the audience's hearing anyway) tells them that Hamlet is to be executed. Though they were clearly shown to be the king's servants and not on Hamlet's "side," they could have thought they were doing no more than taking Hamlet away for the general good of the court. But Hamlet's apparent indifference to their fate sets him up as a man who no longer worries and procrastinates over what he should do, even in life or death situations. Decisiveness has replaced self-doubt. He takes no great relish in the deaths of Rosencrantz and Guildenstern: he is fatalistic about their end and the actions he must take.

Osrick arrives. Although Osrick, Hamlet, and Horatio are "nobles" the blank verse that Hamlet used to tell Horatio what befell him during his absence is instantly replaced by prose; a more suitable form for a comic interlude. Osrick's interview with Hamlet is pure comedy between the back-story Hamlet offers Horatio and the exquisite summing-up of his fatalism at lines 233–238. The comedy consists of two elements: Osrick's affected, flowery language and his confusion at Hamlet's deliberate contradictions.

Once again Shakespeare is demonstrating his skill at another style of writing. Osrick's speech is a pastiche of a type of discourse known as Euphuistic, which originated in a prose work called *Euphus* written by Thomas Lyly and published in 1580. The character of Euphus speaks with exaggerated use of alliteration, antithesis, and classical allusions. The sense of what he is saying is often hidden among all these devices. Osrick accompanies his foppish words with suitable gestures, and on stage his costume usually suggests a vain peacock. The other strand of humor in his meeting with Hamlet is that as a courtier he feels himself required to defer to a prince. So Hamlet's deliberate changes of mind about the temperature leave Osrick unable to say anything sensible.
❍ Where else does Hamlet use his position to drive a social subordinate into confusion?

But Osrick does advance the plot. He sets up the final, fatal confrontation. There is a nice irony in the bloody climax being introduced in a comic scene. It is a measure of Shakespeare's confidence in his own talents as a dramatist that he can stop the dramatic rush towards the play's climax with a long comic interlude which adds nothing to the plot beyond the delivering of an invitation.

There is a great contrast between Hamlet's icily humorous attacks on Osrick's foppery and his philosophical summing up of man's life to Horatio (lines 233–238). Freed from self-doubt, Hamlet has enlarged his view of life and death. He is fatalistic: a man will do whatever it is decreed for him to do. His tone is resigned, but carries a hint of danger. Hamlet is seeing his personal dilemma as just part of a much bigger picture in which his own decisions and wishes play very little part. It is likely that he senses some plot against him is about to be enacted, but he is resigned to seeing how it will turn out. He does not suggest what the plot might be nor how he will react to it, but he knows *The readiness is all* (lines 236–237). This fatalistic approach frees him from the urge to debate with himself over his personal responsibilities. Notice how Hamlet stays in prose in his summing up, whereas most of his previous philosophical meditations have been in blank verse soliloquies.

❂ Lines 233–238 are dramatically crucial to our understanding of Hamlet's character at the end of the play. How would you paraphrase them in a few lines of your own?

The second half of this scene begins with the arrival of Claudius, Gertrude, Laertes, and the rest of the court. But the climax of the play starts rather shakily. Why do the court simply accept that the exile is returned suddenly, now apparently sane? More importantly, what is the point of Hamlet's apology to Laertes? Hamlet may realize that he did Laertes wrong by attacking him at his sister's funeral. Hamlet's view of the inevitability of life and fate may account for him feeling the need to apologize to Laertes, who, it may just turn out, will be harmed by what is about to take place.

Hamlet claims it was not him but his *madness* (line 251) that caused the wrongs Laertes has suffered. He goes to considerable lengths to explain this division between himself and his madness. It throws open the question of whether his madness was real or feigned, but at a point in the plot where this is dramatically irrelevant. Hamlet's apology runs from line 240, *Give me your pardon sir,* to 258, where the concluding image mentions (by inference) the idea that Laertes might be regarded as an accidentally hurt *brother*. Given that we have never seen any relationship between Hamlet and Laertes before, let alone a close, "brotherly" one, Hamlet's apology seems to have little practical relevance to the drama of the play.

The only reason for Hamlet's apology to Laertes must be to paint him as a forgiving and considerate figure before his death: a death in part caused by the chicanery of the man to whom he has just shown such generosity of spirit.

Like the final scene in *King Lear,* the sheer number of deaths can cause humorous comment. It is vital you imagine this scene on stage to understand its dramatic drive and effect. The swordplay is usually quite lengthy: well played, there is space, albeit brief, between the deaths.

Claudius and Gertrude enter together, but Claudius's treachery locks them apart in separate worlds throughout this scene. Claudius has his mind focused totally on the poisoned and unbated sword and on the poisoned cup of wine. He remains the smiling villain: he orders the rules of the bout and appears calm and generous. He presents a perfect picture of a monarch about to enjoy some harmless entertainment at his court.

Gertrude appears to have eyes only for her son. She is proud of this accomplished swordsman, who more importantly seems to have regained both his wits and his social skills. He is her champion. She may be upholding his cause against Laertes purely out of motherly love and pride. But she may also wish to be seen as standing apart from the apparently icy impartiality of Claudius. If she knows of the private conversations that her husband has been having with Laertes, then she may feel that Hamlet needs someone to stand up "on his side." Whatever her feelings, she seems happy to be supporting her son in his innocent bout against Laertes. It is a cruel but perfect dramatic device to have her die by drinking a salute to Hamlet.

Why does Claudius not dash the poisoned cup from Gertrude's lips? His treachery will be revealed, but the woman he loves will be saved. Is it because ultimately he wants to preserve his own life and position? His inaction adds hugely to the depths of his villainy, and we see this only at the very end of his life.

One by one, characters are killed—almost accidentally. But Hamlet does physically revenge his father; he plunges the poisoned sword into Claudius. This long anticipated revenge is not accomplished by a calm Hamlet confronting Claudius with the Ghost's accusations, but by an already dying Hamlet murdering Claudius in a fury after hearing the words of the living, not the dead. Hamlet is striking down Claudius for causing his own imminent death as much as for murdering his father.

Horatio's fond farewell to his dying friend echoes the feelings of most people in the audience. This is tragedy of enormous proportions. Hamlet's death fulfills the requirement of a revenge tragedy: the revenger is condemned and dies by completing the act of revenge. Hamlet's death is swift; he hardly outlives the villain.

The simultaneous arrival of Fortinbras from Poland and the Ambassadors from England (with news of Rosencrantz and Guildenstern's death) is perhaps a little too coincidental for modern minds used to neo-realism in drama, but it is a wonderful expanding of the end of the play from a court tragedy into a national political perspective. Fortinbras, with Hamlet's *dying voice* (line 393) of approval, has finally resolved what has been a background political drama throughout: the balance of power between Denmark and Norway. With fine irony the warlike Fortinbras will take the Danish throne without lifting a finger. Also ironic is the fact that Fortinbras tries to honor Hamlet with what he himself would wish for: a soldier's funeral. But Hamlet was anything but a military, war-like man. It is fortunate that Horatio has been prevented from drinking the dregs of the poison and will, as Hamlet requested, *in this harsh world draw thy breath in pain* to *tell my story* (lines 383–384).

Laughter (sorry, Slaughter) at Elsinore!

? For some the overwhelming feeling at the end of *Hamlet* is of waste. Draw a Mind Map of what has been wasted in both the court and Denmark by the slaughter at the end of the play.

? Imagine you are Horatio, honoring Hamlet's request to speak on his behalf after his death. A visiting ambassador asks for a brief account of what you saw and heard. Make a Mind Map of key events in Hamlet's story that you witnessed and the conversations you had with Hamlet. (Give a step-by-step general picture of the unfolding tragedy as you witnessed it.)

Test your knowledge

? Here are the names of the eight deaths in Hamlet. Beside each say how they died and who killed them (if anyone).

1 Polonius.
2 Ophelia.
3 Rosencrantz.
4 Guildenstern.

5 Gertrude.
6 Claudius.
7 Laertes.
8 Hamlet.

(Answers, see p. 92)

(Answers, see p. 92)

Answers to Test your knowledge

LANGUAGE, STYLE, AND STRUCTURE

1 Old Hamlet, about his murder.
2 Hamlet, about an *honest man.*
3 Hamlet, about mankind.
4 Claudius, about murdering his brother.
5 Hamlet, to Gertrude about her remarriage.
6 Hamlet, to Gertrude about her remarriage.
7 Claudius, about Hamlet's madness.
8 Hamlet, about Polonius's corpse.
9 Gertrude, about Ophelia's mad utterances.
10 First Gravedigger, about dead bodies.

COMMENTARY

ACT 1

1 Barnardo to Horatio.
2 Horatio to the Ghost.
3 Claudius to Laertes.
4 Hamlet to Gertrude.
5 Polonius to Ophelia.
6 The Ghost to Hamlet.
7 Hamlet speaking of Gertrude.
8 Hamlet speaking of Claudius.
9 Hamlet speaking of the Ghost.
10 Hamlet to Horatio and Marcellus.

ACT 2

1 Drinking, fencing, swearing, quarrelling, drabbing.
2 His doublet was *all unbraced,/ No hat upon his head, his stockings fouled,/ Ungartered, and down-gyved to his ankles.*
3 Sending back his letters and refusing to see him.
4 Polonius's announcement of the cause of Hamlet's madness.
5 Hamlet says he reads words and that the matter is slander.
6 Man.
7 A daughter.
8 Polonius.
9 The Players.
10 The devil.

ACT 3

1 Claudius and Polonius.
2 Death.
3 Remembrances.
4 A fool.
5 Ophelia.
6 "The Mousetrap."
7 Kill Claudius.
8 *As kill a king and marry with his brother.*
9 Hamlet.
10 Polonius.

ACT 4

1 (a) Gertrude,   (b) Hamlet.
2 (a) Hamlet,   (b) Polonius.
3 (a) Hamlet,   (b) Fortinbras's army.
4 (a) Horatio,   (b) Ophelia.
5 (a) Gertrude,   (b) the common people.
6 (a) Laertes,   (b) Polonius.
7 (a) Laertes,   (b) Hamlet.
8 (a) Claudius,   (b) Laertes.

ACT 5

1 Stabbed by Hamlet.
2 Kills (drowns) herself.
3 Hanged by the English on orders rewritten by Hamlet.
4 Hanged by the English on orders rewritten by Hamlet.
5 Drinks the cup poisoned by Claudius.
6 Stabbed by Hamlet.
7 Stabbed by Hamlet.
8 Stabbed by Laertes.

Hamlet is the most performed play of all time, ever, anywhere. Not bad for a 400-year-old play written largely in verse! Its complexity means that it has been studied as a text ever since it first appeared in print. It has attracted intense critical interest. Dozens of essays and books have been written about *Hamlet.* This raises a problem for students. It is important to know some of the main critical approaches that have been put forward over the years, but where do you start?

It is not a good idea to go out and read a whole book on the play by one critic. The whole point of studying criticism is to judge and balance opposing views. Just reading one critic's viewpoint will not really help you do this. You need to gain an overview of what people have thought. This section gives you a very quick run-through of the history of criticism of *Hamlet.*

The problem of Hamlet's delay

Delay is a crucial part of any revenge tragedy. If the revenger does the deed directly after being told about the need for it by the ghost, then there's not much of a play! The eighteenth-century critic Thomas Hanmer was the first to point this out. Up until then audiences had probably just accepted that even the most blood-curdling revenge hero had to delay a while just because that was how revenge tragedy worked. But ever since Hanmer, critics have puzzled over possible deeper meanings in Hamlet's delay. Many have looked for psychological reasons.

Hamlet was the fictional darling of the Romantic Movement (a literary movement influential in the period 1770–1845). The Romantic sensibility saw the convergence of two of their favorite themes in Hamlet: the alienated individual and madness. So much was said and written about Hamlet at this time that he was in danger of becoming mistaken for a real person instead of a fictional creation. Many other writers felt a great kinship with the intellectual, socially isolated Danish prince. The character of Hamlet was often more important to commentators of this period than the play as a dramatic whole.

Some critics said that the play was so complex and loaded with meaning that it was better to read it on the page than see it performed on stage. This might be thought a strange opinion to hold about a play that was written to be performed before what the Romantics would no doubt have considered a rough and insensitive Elizabethan audience.

It is important to remember that Shakespeare was a man of the theater, and an actor himself. As far as we can judge he wrote his plays remarkably quickly and they were equally speedily made ready for performance. He was not laboring slowly and painfully to produce intellectual masterpieces for critics to puzzle over. He was a popular writer busy in the turmoil of Elizabethan theater.

The psychology of characters

Critics in the nineteenth and early twentieth centuries continued to look more at characters than the play as a whole drama. As well as Hamlet, Claudius, Gertrude, and Ophelia became subjects of intense speculation in essays examining their psychology.

Hamlet's delay in taking revenge was still a problem. Critics considered whether Claudius, when as it were off-stage, was so well guarded, and so aware of Hamlet's plans, that Hamlet could not make a move. There is nothing in the text to suggest this!

Because so many critics were digging through the play hoping to prove their arguments, it developed (among scholars at least) a reputation for being difficult. But for actors it remained the play that offered them some of the greatest roles in theater. Audiences flocked to enjoy the drama. But critical objections to the play reached a new height with the famous poet T. S. Eliot's essay on the play in 1919. Eliot said it was a failure because, in the character of Hamlet, Shakespeare was trying to explore a disgust for life that he, the author, didn't understand. Gertrude hasn't really done anything that should logically cause such horror and revulsion to her son. Eliot's extreme view is hardly defensible: if the play were a failure why has it been so popular and caused so much critical inquiry for nearly four centuries? But there have been times when anything Shakespeare wrote has been regarded as sacrosanct by some critics. Eliot's attack did bring some fresh air into the debate.

With the development of psychoanalysis at the beginning of the twentieth century, critics had a new range of psychological concepts and a vocabulary to discuss Hamlet and the rest of the cast in more detail. One critic, Ernest Jones, seems to be more like a doctor writing case notes on his patients than a critic looking at a piece of drama. He claimed (in 1949) that Hamlet's unhealthy obsession with his mother's sexuality renders him unable to commit violence against Claudius for in murdering Old Hamlet, Claudius has done what Hamlet subconsciously wanted to do himself.

Critical theories of the late twentieth century

Structuralists see all pieces of literature as constructions of language, not scripts or stories. Their approach is strictly scholarly and has nothing to do with the world of theater and performance, where *Hamlet* is still regarded as essentially a script, albeit one of the greatest ever written. Structuralist critics look for occurrences of key words through the text. These words relate to each other in ways that create links and forces that are not apparent to the ordinary reader.

Post-structuralists take this code idea even further. For them there is no one correct meaning in the text; not even the one Shakespeare intended. *Hamlet* is a puzzle made up of language that can have endless different meanings. No one meaning is better or more valid than any other. (Not very helpful if you are an actor trying to realize a part or a director trying to make the play come alive on stage!)

Feminist critics often apply a standard template to artworks: how the piece demonstrates the sexual stereotyping that exists in wider society. Feminist critics have seen Gertrude and Ophelia as women silenced by males. They have looked at possible reasons why they have far fewer lines than the male characters. Another major focus of much of their criticism has been trying to identify what divides the character of Hamlet from the females in the play.

You may well feel that much contemporary criticism has very little to do with the play and much to do with critics using what is probably the most famous text in theater as a platform for exploring their own theories. It is a testament to the greatness and universality of the story *Hamlet* tells that the text has been used by so many diverse critics and scholars to prove different theories, some of which seem only marginally to do with the script an Elizabethan playwright wrote for his company of actors!

 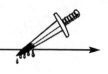

Hamlet's soliloquy, Act 2, scene 2, lines 576–634

This soliloquy closes a long and event-packed scene in which we have seen Hamlet feigning madness for the first time. Because of his *antic disposition* it is possible to lose sight of his real state of mind. This speech serves to reveal it to us, and to prepare us for the action of the next Act. The soliloquy is written almost entirely in blank verse. Shorter lines (585, 610, 616) are used to close specific sections within it. Each one has an exclamation mark to heighten the closing effect.

As if to emphasize Hamlet's clear and logical thinking underneath the show of emotion, the soliloquy divides into six sections. Each is a separate train of thought. The order is logical: one section's content leads naturally onto the next.

576–586: Hamlet describes the passion of the Player.

586–593: He imagines the excesses of emotion the Player would exhibit if he had Hamlet's motives to be moved.

594–609: Hamlet berates himself for lack of action. He imagines an invisible foe deriding and abusing him. He rises to a fury against this *villain.*

610–616: Suddenly aware of the hollowness in this display of frustrated passion, he compares himself to an insincere whore.

617–627: He explains his plan to judge Claudius's guilt by his reaction to the play.

627–634: He explains he needs more positive proof because the Ghost may have been a disguised devil.

The soliloquy opens with Hamlet's cursing himself as a *rogue and peasant slave* (line 576). *Peasant* is commonly used by Shakespeare as a term of abuse. Hamlet goes on to explain this outburst of self-hatred. It links to what has just gone before: the First Player moving himself to tears when reciting a speech.

Hamlet has far more reason to be moved to passion than the actor, but he cannot shake off his caution and melancholy. This is the phase of the play where Hamlet has been urged to seek revenge but finds himself constantly questioning whether he should act. His intellect, which is getting in the way of decisive action, is brilliantly displayed in the soliloquy.

He describes how the actor cried tears for *Hecuba* over her murdered husband. The fact that her story is taken from antiquity emphasizes the distance between the actor and the cause of his emotion. It is *a dream of passion* (line 579). Hamlet describes the appearance of the moved and tearful Player (lines 581–584). This description is brought to a close by the short line *For Hecuba!* (line 585). Breaking the iambic rhythm here denotes a climax in Hamlet's thoughts. Repeating her name in the following line reinforces this.

Hamlet compares his own position to the Player's. He imagines the absurd excesses of passion the Player would display if he had Hamlet's reasons to be moved. *He would drown the stage with tears* (line 589), his anguish would *Make mad the guilty and appal the free* (line 591). This is not as straightforward as it might seem. Elizabethan audiences saw it as an essential part of an actor's art that they displayed passion they didn't really feel. So by comparing himself to an actor Hamlet is not making an entirely fair comparison of his emotional inertia and the actor's tears. Notice also the use of *guilty* in line 591: Hamlet may be thinking here of the effect of such passion on Claudius, guilty of the murder. He may be thinking ahead to the play.

At the end of line 593 Hamlet turns his critical gaze back upon himself. His language is rich with immediate and striking images. He is *a dull and muddy-mettled rascal* (line 594). This image combines the idea of being dull-spirited with metal that has lost its shine. He is like *John-a-Dreams* (line 595), a nickname for a dreamy, ineffectual person.

At line 598 he moves on again; questioning himself, asking if he is a coward. His anger is such that he appears to be challenging some invisible accuser who calls him *a villain* (line 599). There is a series of images of physical attack: *pate* or head hitting, nose and beard pulling. *The lie i'th'throat / As deep as to the lungs* (lines 601–602) suggests a lie that is no mere slip of the tongue. When in a fury he asks who commits these imaginary wrongs upon him, we can imagine Hamlet in a useless frenzy: there is no one there to answer. The anger that fuels the speech up to now is all born of frustration with his own inability to act.

He forces himself to admit that he is a coward: *pigeon-livered* and *lacking gall/ To make oppression bitter* (lines 604–605). He cannot turn the anger, the *oppression* he feels, into something bitter enough to spur him into action. He should kill Claudius and feed his guts (*offal*) to carrion birds. The *villain* he accuses (lines 606–607) is both Claudius and himself. As before, a short line, a simple cry for vengeance, cuts short this train of thought (line 610).

The soliloquy then changes both pace and focus. His self-hatred is more moderate: he is *an ass* (line 611) not *a rogue and peasant slave.* Imagine this on stage: the actor reaches a violent, emotional climax at *O, vengeance!*, then allows the more rational intellectual side of Hamlet to emerge and look at things more calmly. Lines 611–616 lay out Hamlet's case for action. Then he compares himself to a whore (*a drab*) who falls *a-cursing* (line 615). A wronged whore, being a woman entrapped and usually powerless, can only curse at those who do her wrong. Hamlet feels the same sense of powerlessness.

Hamlet is aware he is revealing his heart and feelings, but in words not deeds. He doubts even the sincerity of what he has just uttered to himself. This is Hamlet coolly analyzing what he has said in passion moments before, and again judging himself unfavorably. This stage in Hamlet's thoughts ends with another slightly shorter line: *A scullion! Fie upon't, foh!* (line 616). *Scullion* is another term for kitchen servant. In some editions *scullion* is replaced by *stallion*, a prostitute, and that derogatory reference follows on from other lines.

The next section of the soliloquy returns us from Hamlet's lengthy self-examination back to the onward progress of the drama. We know the "play within a play" is to be performed the next day. We know Hamlet is plotting to insert extra lines and to use the play as a further (final?) means of testing for his uncle's guilt. Lines 617–634 are straightforward exposition. Hamlet explains the theory that people guilty of crimes can be made to reveal or confess their wrongs by seeing theatrical versions of them enacted on stage. We learn that Hamlet has chosen "The Murder of Gonzago" because it features a murder identical to Claudius's strange way of killing Old Hamlet. We also learn that Hamlet is going to watch Claudius for his reaction and so determine whether to pursue his revenge: *If he do blench,/ I'll know my course* (lines 626–627). We are being readied for what will happen at the impending performance.

After all this clear and positive planning by Hamlet, there is a return to his previous caution. He picks up the idea first mentioned by Horatio in Act 1, scene 4: that the Ghost might be a devil merely adopting the form of Hamlet's father, *and the devil hath power/ T'assume a pleasing shape* (lines 628–629). Why should a devil bother to do this? The answer is not in the supernatural but in the psychological. Hamlet sees that his *weakness* and *melancholy* could have allowed him to fall prey to such deceptions. While the tone of this explanation (lines 630–632) still suggests that a weak mind can easily fall prey to invasion by a devil, there is a feeling that Shakespeare is touching on psychological issues that would not be accepted for many years to come: that the devil may be in Hamlet's head and not a visitor from Hell.

By gauging Claudius's reaction when he sees the play, Hamlet feels he will have *grounds/ More relative* (lines 632–633) to judge the rightness of revenge. So far he only has the word of the Ghost. He want something more definite, more directly connected to events on this earth. The rhyming couplet that concludes this scene neatly sums up Hamlet's plan.

HOW TO GET AN "A" IN ENGLISH LITERATURE

In all your study, in coursework, and in exams, be aware of the following:

- **Characterization**—the characters and how we know about them (e.g. speech, actions, author description), their relationships, and how they develop.
- **Plot and structure**—story and how it is organized into parts or episodes.
- **Setting and atmosphere**—the changing physical scene and how it reflects the story (e.g., a storm reflecting chaos).
- **Style and language**—the author's choice of words, and literary devices such as imagery, and how these reflect the **mood**.
- **Viewpoint**—how the story is told (e.g., through an imaginary narrator, or in the third person but through the eyes of one character—"She was furious—how dare he!").
- **Social and historical context**—the author's influences (see Context).
- **Critical approaches**—different ways in which the text has been, or could be, interpreted.

Develop your ability to:

- Relate **detail** to **broader content, meaning, and style**.
- Show understanding of the author's **intentions, technique, and meaning** (brief and appropriate comparisons with other works by the same author will earn credit).
- Give **personal response and interpretation**, backed up by **examples** and short **quotations**.
- **Evaluate** the author's achievement (how far does the author succeed—give reasons).

Make sure you:

- Use **paragraphs** and **sentences** correctly.
- Write in an appropriate **tone**—formal but not stilted.
- Use short, appropriate quotations as **evidence** of your understanding.
- Use **literary terms** correctly to explain how an author achieves effects.

THE EXAM ESSAY

PLANNING

Your essay is very important. It is worth spending 5–10 minutes planning it. An excellent way to do this is in the three stages below.

1 **Mind Map** your ideas, without worrying about their order yet.
2 **Order** the relevant ideas (the ones that really relate to the question) by numbering them in the order in which you will write the essay.
3 **Gather** your evidence and short quotes.

You could remember this as the **MOG** technique.

WRITING AND CHECKING

Then write the essay, allowing five minutes at the end for checking relevance, spelling, grammar, and punctuation.

REMEMBER!

Stick to the question and always **back up** your points with evidence in the form of examples and short quotations. Note: you can use "…" for unimportant words missed out in a quotation.

MODEL ANSWER AND PLAN

The next (and final) chapter consists of an answer to an exam question on *Hamlet*, with the Mind Map and plan used to write it. Don't be put off if you think you couldn't write an essay like this yet. You'll develop your skills if you work at them. Even if you're reading this the night before the exam, you can easily memorize the MOG technique in order to do your personal best.

The model answer and plan are good examples to follow, but don't learn them by heart. It's better to pay close attention to the wording of the question you choose to answer, and allow Mind Mapping to help you to think creatively and structurally.

Before reading the answer, you might like to do a plan of your own to compare with the example. The numbered points, with comments at the end, show why it's a good answer.

MODEL ANSWER AND ESSAY PLAN

There are many possible themes to write about when considering Shakespeare's tragedy *Hamlet*. Essay themes may include:

1 Hamlet's fatal flaw—his inability to act swiftly, his *hesitancy and indecision* after being charged by his father to avenge his death.
2 Hamlet is a play about *revenge*. The desire to get revenge for his father's death motivates Hamlet to act—eventually. Laertes, too, is motivated by a desire to get revenge for his father's death.
3 *Madness*. Hamlet pretends to be mad while Ophelia's madness is genuine.
4 *The position of women* in the play. What importance do women have to the plot of *Hamlet*?
5 The theme of *actors and acting*. This theme is discussed below with an outline, Mind Map, and model answer.

QUESTION

Shakespeare once said: "All the world's a stage/ And all the men and women merely players" (*As You Like It* Act II Scene 7). Themes of acting and actors are extremely important in Shakespeare's tragedy *Hamlet*, which not only includes a "play within a play" but also the idea of characters acting to disguise their true feelings and motives. Discuss how ideas of actors and acting fill the play.

PLAN

This question asks you to look at the whole play. You should identify two main themes involving acting: mention of actual actors and players, and the idea of characters acting in order that they do not reveal their true selves. The Mind Map identifies the key elements of each theme you should include in your answer.

Your notes or outline may look like this:

1 The opening paragraph contains the thesis, or main idea, of your essay and gives the title and author of the work of

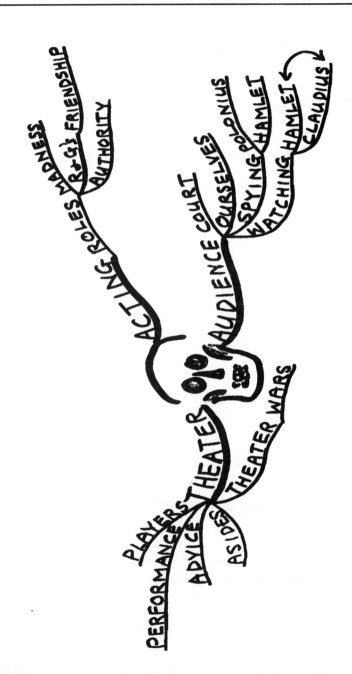

literature you are writing about—in this case the importance of actors and acting in *Hamlet* by William Shakespeare.

2   The first body paragraph gives the setting of, and a brief introduction to, *Hamlet*. This paragraph then discusses "the play within a play" and its importance to the plot of *Hamlet*.

3   The second body paragraph discusses the idea of how characters can "act a part" in order to hide their true intentions. This paragraph gives specific examples from the play.

4   The third body paragraph discusses ideas about audience and spectators and spying.

5   The concluding paragraph discusses how all the above details support the thesis that in *Hamlet* ideas about actors and acting have great importance.

A NOTE ON QUOTES

Use your knowledge of the text to support your ideas. Never use quotes as padding: say why you are using them, what point you are illustrating, and explain them if the meaning is not absolutely clear. Use quotes as examples when discussing the style and imagery of the passage. Avoid simply paraphrasing.

You will find that making a Mind Map of the main elements you need to include in your answer will help you focus on the important points and stop you getting sidetracked into considering things that are not actually required to answer the question. Make the Mind Map and essay outline before you begin to write. Your Mind Map should look something like the one on p. 105.

ESSAY

The themes of actors and acting fill Shakespeare's tragedy *Hamlet* and are vitally important to the play. In *Hamlet* Shakespeare reveals his fascination with, and knowledge of, all things theatrical. As he once wrote: "All the world's a stage/And all the men and women merely players." Not only is there a "play within a play," which forms a core part of the plot, but the characters themselves often act to disguise their true feelings and emotions. The idea of playing to an audience is also explored, whether it is to the general audience of the play or characters within the play acting to deceive other characters. An example of this is when Hamlet feigns madness.

Set in Denmark in the Dark Ages, the play is essentially a revenge tragedy in which Hamlet, the young prince, is called upon by his father's ghost to avenge his (Old Hamlet's) brutal murder at the hands of Claudius. The most obvious use of actors and acting in the play is in Act 2 scene 2 when Hamlet instructs the traveling players to stage "The Murder of Gonzago" (which Hamlet also refers to as "The Mousetrap") for the court the following evening. This play depicts a murder identical to the one the Ghost said was perpetrated on him; Hamlet uses this device to test the guilt of Claudius, who will be in the audience. When the play is actually performed (in Act 3) Claudius storms out, thus confirming Hamlet's suspicions. As Hamlet says:

> *The play's the thing*
> *Wherein I'll catch the conscience of the King*

Hamlet marvels at the player's ability to feign emotion and weep at will:

> *What's Hecuba to him or he to Hecuba*
> *That he should weep for her?*

In his interactions with the players Hamlet reveals his knowledge of, and respect for, the power of acting. The "play within a play" scene is multi-layered: during it Hamlet is both a member of the audience and an actor himself. He is playing the part of a madman and watching not only the Players but Claudius too.

As well as the Players, many of the main characters in Hamlet may be seen as "acting" a part. Claudius, who has murdered his brother, acts the part of a calm and confident ruler while Gertrude, who has married her dead husband's brother, is regarded by her son as only a "most *seeming-*virtuous queen," which suggests that Hamlet feels she is hiding her true emotions. Rosencrantz and Guildenstern try unsuccessfully to maintain an appearance of friendship with Hamlet while acting as agents for the king. But the most important "actor" of them all is Hamlet, who in Act 1, scene 1 reveals that he intends, "To put an antic disposition on" and feign madness in order to confuse the court about his true intentions. In this guise as a madman Hamlet berates Ophelia about the frailty of women (Act 3, scene 1) and orders her to

"Get thee to a nunnery" knowing all the time that he is being overheard by Claudius and Polonious, whom he wants to consider him mad. Just as when he ordered the Players to act "The Mousetrap," Hamlet is using the power of acting to further his own ends.

Actors, whether professional or merely people acting a part, require an audience—people who look on and observe the action. The idea of spectating or watching others—even spying on them—is used as a plot device in *Hamlet*. Polonious, who, in Act 3, scene 4, hides behind a curtain in Gertrude's private chambers in order to eavesdrop on Hamlet's conversation with his mother, is stabbed to death by Hamlet. Rosencrantz and Guildenstern, whom Claudius had asked to spy on Hamlet, also come to a bad end. In *Hamlet*, with its web of hidden desires and plots, Shakespeare shows that everything might not be as it seems.

The plot and characters of *Hamlet* certainly reveal how important ideas of actors and acting were to Shakespeare and this play supports Shakespeare's contention that "All the world's a stage." In Hamlet not only the "play within a play" but the actions of many of the main characters reveal that, in art as in life, we all have our parts to play and appearances may well be deceiving.

WHAT'S SO GOOD ABOUT THIS ANSWER?

1 The opening paragraph establishes the main idea of the essay and gives the title and author. It discusses the idea of actors and acting in *Hamlet*.

2 The first body paragraph develops in more detail how Shakespeare uses the "play within a play" as a plot device.

3 The second body paragraph expands on the idea that characters in Hamlet may be seen to be "acting" parts. It gives specific examples from the text.

4 The third body paragraph develops the idea of "audience" and also of spying.

5 The conclusion ties all the ideas together to prove the thesis that *Hamlet* is indeed filled with ideas about actors and acting.

6 The essay shows a thorough knowledge of all aspects of the play but avoids plot summary.

7 The essay uses quotations and specific references from the text to support the ideas it puts forward.

8 The essay is logically presented in well-organized paragraphs.

9 The tone of the essay is suitable to its intended audience.

10 The essay obeys the conventions of standard written English.

11 In summary, this essay is a thoughtful, insightful response to the suggested topic, showing a thorough knowledge of themes in *Hamlet* and the importance of ideas about actors and acting to the play.

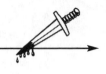

GLOSSARY OF LITERARY TERMS

alliteration   the repetition, for effect, of consonant sounds.

allusion   the use of literary, cultural, and historical references.

antithesis   combining contrasting ideas or images for dramatic effect.

assonance   the repetition, for effect, of vowel sounds.

classical allusions   referring to characters or events in ancient Greek and Roman literature.

context   the background of social, historical, and literary influences on a work.

diction   choice and arrangement of words.

didactic   intended to instruct; in literary criticism, often used in negative sense.

discursive   presenting a logical argument, step by step.

exposition   the laying out of the situation from which the plot develops. It can be direct, with a chorus or figure not involved in the action explaining the background, or indirect, as in *Hamlet*, where the situation is revealed in conversations between characters.

feminist criticism   critical approach developed in the 1960s, based on assessing the role of gender in texts. A particular issue is the subordination of women in a patriarchal society.

genre   type of literary work conforming to certain expectations; e.g., tragedy.

groundlings   members of the Elizabethan and Jacobean theater audience who stood in the pit or floor area in front of the stage. (Also known as "stinkards!")

iambic   two-syllable "foot" or unit of poetry, consisting of an unstressed syllable followed by a stressed one. (See also *pentameter*.)

idiom   a characteristic expression of a language or *dialect*.

image a word picture bringing an idea to life by appealing to the senses.

Latinate stemming from Latin.

Marxist criticism critical approach which sees literature in relation to class struggle, and assesses the way texts present social realities.

melodrama style of drama that appeals to sentiments and passions, usually lacking subtlety.

metaphor a compressed *simile* describing something as if it were something else; e.g., Hamlet describes the night sky as *this majestical roof fretted with golden fire* (Act 2, scene 2, lines 324–325).

onomatopoeia use of words whose sound imitates the thing they describe.

parody an exaggerated copy (especially of a writer's style) made for humorous effect.

pastiche an imitation of another style (of writing), often exaggerated.

pentameter line of poetry consisting of ten syllables. The iambic pentameter (see *iambic*) is the standard line of poetry used by Shakespeare in his plays.

persona an assumed identity.

personification an *image* speaking of something abstract, such as love, death or sleep, as if it were a person or a god.

plot the story; the events that take place and how they are arranged.

polemical (of style) making an argument.

rhetorical expressed with a view to persuade (often used in negative sense).

satire literature which humorously exposes and ridicules vice and folly.

simile an *image* comparing two things similar in some way but different in others, normally using "like" or "as"; e.g., Hamlet describes man as being *like an angel* (Act 2, scene 2, lines 329–330).

Structuralism   school of critical thought which sees all texts as codes of language.

structure   the organization of a text; e.g., narrative, plot, repeated images, and symbols.

subplot   subsidiary plot coinciding with the main plot and often reflecting aspects of it.

tone   the mood created by a writer's choice and organization of words; e.g., persuasive.

viewpoint   the way a narrator approaches the material and the audience.

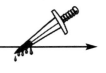

back-story 6–7
Barnardo 41, 44
blank verse 36
Claudius
  character 15–17, 74–75
  as conspirator 79–80, 89–90
  death 90
  guilt 16–17, 66, 67–69
  as king 15–16, 43, 59, 62,
    78–79
"Closet scene" 69–73
Euphuistic speech 87
fate 54
feminist criticism 97
Fortinbras 26–27, 89
Francisco 41
Gertrude
  character 17–18, 74–75,
    77–78, 81
  and Hamlet 69–73, 89
Ghost
  appearances 41, 42, 47, 72
  as character 18–19
"Graveyard scene" 82–86
Hamlet
  apology to Laertes 88–89
  character 11–15
  death 90
  delay 48, 57, 69, 94–95
  "facts" 12
  honor 13–14, 68–69
  madness 13, 48, 53–54, 73,
    75–76
  melancholy 13, 44, 48, 53, 57,
    83–84
  Oedipal tendency 12–13,
    70–73
  popular public figure 79
  and sexuality 14–15, 61–62, 64
  soliloquies 44, 60–61, 76–77
  and suicide 44, 60
Horatio 24–25, 41, 42, 44, 47,
  48, 49, 63, 79

imagery 38
Laertes
  character 22–23
  death 90
  and revenge 78–79, 80, 85
Marcellus 41, 44, 46, 47, 48
"Murder of Gonzago" 33–34, 57,
  64, 65–66
Ophelia
  character 23–24, 45–46, 51,
    61–62
  death 81
  madness 77–78
Osrick 26, 87
Players 55, 56–57, 63
poetry and prose 36–37, 51,
  60–61, 62, 63, 80, 83
politics 41, 52–53
Polonius
  character 19–22
  as comic figure 19–21, 53, 56,
    64
  as courtier 52–53, 59, 62
  death 71
  as parent 19, 21, 45–46,
    50–51, 62
purgatory 47–48
revenge tragedy 3, 49
Reynaldo 50–51
Rosencrantz and Guildenstern
  25–26, 54, 66, 67, 75–76
sources 1–3
structuralist criticism 96–97
Themes
  Corruption 32–33
  Madness 31–32
  Mortality 33
  Revenge 30
  Theater 33–34
  Words and actions 30–31
"War of the Theatres" 54–55
Yorick 84